THE CURRY SECRET

Also available

An Indian Housewife's Recipe Book
Chinese Cookery Secrets

THE CURRY SECRET

INDIAN RESTAURANT COOKERY AT HOME

Kris Dhillon

A HOW TO BOOK

ROBINSON

ROBINSON

Originally published in the UK in 1989

This new completely revised and updated edition
published by Robinson in 2008

Copyright © Kris Dhillon, 1989, 2008

12

All rights reserved.
No part of this publication may be reproduced, stored in a retrieval system, or
transmitted, in any form, or by any means, without the prior permission in writing
of the publisher, nor be otherwise circulated in any form of binding or cover other
than that in which it is published and without a similar condition including this
condition being imposed on the subsequent purchaser.

A CIP catalogue record for this book
is available from the British Library.

ISBN: 978-0-7160-2191-9

Printed and bound in Great Britain by Clays Ltd., St Ives plc

Papers used by Robinson are from well-managed forests
and other responsible sources

Robinson
An imprint of
Little, Brown Book Group
Carmelite House
50 Victoria Embankment
London EC4Y 0DZ

An Hachette UK Company
www.hachette.co.uk

www.littlebrown.co.uk

How To Books are published by Robinson, an imprint of Little, Brown Book Group.
We welcome proposals from authors who have first-hand experience of their subjects.
Please set out the aims of your book, its target market and its suggested contents in
an email to Nikki.Read@howtobooks.co.uk

CONTENTS

INTRODUCTION

Many difficulties stand in the way of anyone trying to explore the secrets of Indian restaurant cooking. People buy an Indian cookbook but find that the traditional recipes and methods can be disappointing when they produce a home-cooked taste and not the distinct flavour of restaurant curries. This is not really surprising as the art of restaurant cooking is a very closely kept secret, next to impossible to uncover.

A top chef guards his trade secrets closely, knowing that he may become dispensable should the proprietor acquire his skills. A proprietor who is also the chef aims to satisfy his customers, but also keeps his knowledge close to his heart.

At the risk of upsetting my contemporaries, I have chosen to reveal all. The following pages will show you simply and precisely how to create the curries you love, in your own kitchen, using the same techniques as your favourite restaurants. Secret recipes, special little 'tricks of the trade', have all been included to give you the knowledge to reproduce that special taste that, until now, may well have eluded you.

Weights and Measures
Both metric and imperial measurements have been given in this book with the metric measures being rounded up or down to the nearest unit. Remember to use one or the other and not to combine imperial and metric measurements in one recipe.

All spoon measurements throughout the book are slightly rounded spoonfuls unless specified as being level.

I refer to two types of 'cup' measurement in the recipes. The first, which I call the 'UK cup', is the size of a UK teacup, approximately 5 fluid ounces or 150ml. The second is the standard US cup: 8 fluid ounces or 240ml. The important thing is that you use the same cup size throughout a recipe.

1

SPICES AND HERBS

The curries in this book require quantities of the following spices and herbs, so it is essential to get these together and to prepare them as suggested before you begin cooking. I think it is safe to say that most supermarkets and grocers now stock these items. Ethnic grocers will certainly have supplies of both fresh and dry ingredients available all year round.

Other than for rice dishes, restaurants do not generally use spices in their whole form. However, they will buy them whole and then grind small quantities at a time for the best flavour. I suggest in general that you follow this example. An electric coffee-grinder is ideal for the grinding as it grinds the spices to the fineness required for restaurant curries. (Alternatively, you could use a pestle and mortar.) This degree of fineness is not of particular importance for home cooking, but a restaurant chef is meticulous in this requirement and will test the ground spices between forefinger and thumb, being satisfied only when the mixture feels perfectly smooth. This is quite a task with the amounts used for a busy restaurant, but easy enough when grinding a few tablespoonfuls at home.

When storing the dry ingredients, use glass or plastic containers with well-fitting lids and keep in a cool, dry place away from strong light. Whole spices will keep their flavour for months when stored in this way. Remember to label all your containers clearly as it is extremely difficult to tell which spice is which after they have been ground.

For those of you who are new to Indian cooking, the following descriptions should be helpful when buying the spices and herbs you will need.

Amchoor/Amchur

This is a powder made from dried green mangoes and has a unique sweet and sour taste. Buy small quantities as you will require relatively little of this ingredient.

Bay leaves

These will be familiar to cooks as they are used for flavouring all sorts of dishes of many different origins. In Indian cooking we use them whole for rice dishes and grind them with other ingredients to make garam masala.

Cardamoms (green)

Small, whitish green pods full of dark, sweetly aromatic seeds. Used in sweet and savoury dishes.

Cardamoms (black)

Larger than their green counterparts, these are dark brown in colour with a stronger flavour and aroma. They are an important ingredient in garam masala.

Chillies (green)

These vary in length from about 1 inch (2.5cm) to about 4 inches (10cm), have dark green flesh and flat, round white seeds. Generally speaking, the small chillies have a tendency to be hotter than the larger ones so they will work out more economical. Besides providing the heat in Indian foods, green chillies impart a special flavour not found with the dried red chillies.

Store whole and unwashed in paper, and place in the salad compartment of a refrigerator.

Freezing: Grind in a blender or food processor with a little water and freeze in ice-cube trays. Fresh green chillies are past their best after a week or so, so this is a good idea if you cook Indian food infrequently.

NB. Handle cut chillies very carefully as the irritant in them will cause a burning sensation on contact with skin. Always wash your hands before touching your face.

Chillies (red powder)

Chilli powder adds colour to Indian curries as well as heat and flavour. Unlike other dry ingredients which are best bought whole, I recommend that you buy these ready ground as chilli powder. The reason for this is that grinding red chillies requires particular care as the fine powder will escape to irritate eyes, nose, and throat, causing terrible bouts of sneezing and runny eyes.

Cinnamon

Buy sticks, as pieces of cinnamon are used in rice dishes. It is ground with other spices in garam masala.

Cloves
These are used for their flavour and aroma, whole in rice dishes and ground for garam masala.

Coriander (fresh green)
This is easily the most wonderful, versatile, and widely used herb of all in Indian cooking, both in the home and the restaurant. Commercially grown coriander is taller – growing to some 10 inches (25cm) or so – than the home-grown variety and is readily available from ethnic grocers and greengrocers. The flavour and aroma of this lovely herb makes it a vital ingredient for turning a good Indian dish into an excellent one, whether stirred into a curry or sprinkled onto hot food as a garnish.

Use leaves and stems and chop finely (discarding any tough pieces) and add to food right at the end of cooking as the delicate flavour is easily lost.

Fresh coriander will keep for a week or so if you immerse the stems in a container of water just as you would a bunch of flowers.

Coriander seeds
As delicate in flavour as the plant from which they come, these seeds are small, round, and beige in colour. In the restaurant, coriander is ground and used as a spice in its own right as well as in garam masala.

Cumin seeds
These look like caraway seeds, have quite a strong flavour, and are used in the restaurant mostly in their ground form.

Cumin seeds (black)
Finer and darker than regular cumin, this spice is also more expensive. It is unlikely that you will find black cumin in supermarkets, so you may have to go to an Asian grocer. If you cannot get it, you may use regular cumin as a substitute.

Fenugreek (dry leaves)
Not to be confused with fenugreek seeds, this is a dark green leafy plant similar in height to coriander. The flavour is not as subtle as that of coriander and becomes more concentrated when the plant is dried. Known as 'methi' it is available from Asian grocers in both its fresh and dry form. It is the dry ingredient that is used in restaurant cooking and, although fenugreek is perhaps not an essential herb for restaurant curries, it certainly adds that 'extra something' so is worth trying if you can get it.

To prepare for use, pick out and discard any straw-like pieces. Grind in a coffee-grinder, sieve, and store in a glass jar. Do not forget to label.

Garlic

A familiar and popular herb, garlic is particularly necessary for the flavour of restaurant curries where it is used in generous amounts. Buy bulbs that have firm, plump cloves, and store in a cool, dry place as you would onions.

Ginger (fresh)

This looks like a thick, knobbly root. Scraping away the pale brown skin reveals a creamy yellow, slightly fibrous interior. The fresher the ginger, the less fibrous it tends to be, so to ensure freshness, look for plump pieces with a taut skin.

To store, keep in a cool, dry, airy place as you would other vegetables.

Freezing: Peel and grind into a paste with a little water and freeze in ice-cube trays. You can then take out a cube or two as you require it.

Nutmeg

Nutmegs can be bought from supermarkets as well as from Asian grocers. Buy whole, and break into pieces by hitting lightly with a hammer or rolling pin before grinding.

Paprika

A personal favourite, paprika is excellent for adding colour and a very slightly tangy/sweet flavour to curries. It can be bought in small tins with tight-fitting plastic lids which is an ideal way of storing this spice. If buying in polythene bags, transfer to a glass jar and label, as it is difficult to distinguish between paprika and chilli powder without tasting.

Turmeric

This spice is used in Asian cooking mainly for its yellow colour although it also aids the digestion and has a mild, earthy flavour. Buy turmeric that is a bright yellow colour and handle carefully as it will stain hands and clothes.

GARAM MASALA

The *garam* means 'hot' and the *masala* a 'mixture of spices', so this is a hot spice mixture. The heat, however, is not a heat that you taste as with chillies, but one that affects the body. This theory originates from the Hindu concept of medicine and diet called *tridosha*, which teaches that some foods have a warming effect on the body while others have a cooling one. Spices such as cloves, cinnamon, black cardamoms, and nutmeg are *garam* constituents of this aromatic mixture.

The garam masala should be added to foods towards the end of cooking and is sometimes also sprinkled onto cooked meat, vegetables and yogurts as a garnish.

How to Make Garam Masala

This makes about 3 tablespoonfuls.

1 tbsp coriander seeds
1 tbsp cumin
1 tsp green cardamoms
1 tsp cloves
1 tsp black peppercorns
2 sticks of cinnamon, about 2 inches (5cm) in length
2 bay leaves
½ small nutmeg
4 black cardamoms

Place all the ingredients into an electric coffee-grinder and grind for 1 minute. Carefully remove the lid and test by rubbing a little of the mixture between forefinger and thumb. Finely ground spices should not feel gritty. If necessary, switch on the machine for another few seconds.

Put the garam masala into a small airtight container, preferably made of glass or plastic, and label.

There are various other mixtures and condiments used in this book which I feel may require explanation.

Chat masala

'Chaat' (the original Indian spelling) or 'chat' (as it's now commonly spelt in the West) literally means 'to lick'. Chat masala is a spice mix that is irresistibly tasty and likely to make you want to lick clean any dish made with it. Dishes that use chat masala are known as 'chats'. Chat masala is available from Asian grocers in small boxes.

Food colourings

These are used quite widely in restaurant cooking. Buy the powdered rather than the liquid variety for greater potency.

Vegetable ghee

This is used mainly for making the rice dishes and the only other suitable alternative is the ghee made from clarifying butter. Something I have found particularly good if you do not wish to do this, and cannot get vegetable ghee, is concentrated butter. This is readily available from supermarkets and shops.

2

SNACKS AND NIBBLES

Indian restaurants do not serve snacks as such but rather what might be called little nibbles that are eaten with a drink while waiting for your meal. These tasty morsels are, however, very popular, so I have included them as I feel that no book on restaurant cooking would be complete without them.

I have, as promised, included the 'tricks of the trade' required to produce the appearance and flavour typical of Indian food.

BOMBAY MIX

This is a mixture of nuts, besan sticks, and spices served to customers in bowls to enjoy with their aperitifs. It is somewhat time-consuming and fiddly to make, and to my knowledge restaurants do not make it themselves. As bought varieties are excellent, I feel it unnecessary to go to the time and trouble of making it yourself. Bombay mix is readily available from delicatessens, healthfood stores, shops and supermarkets, as well as Asian grocers.

POPADOMS

The restaurant method of cooking popadoms will produce far better results than the usual method of simply frying which can leave the popadoms rather greasy.

Please read the instructions carefully and have all the utensils ready before you begin.

Plain and/or spicy popadoms
Vegetable oil for frying

Heat the oil in a large, deep frying pan until very hot but not smoking.

Take TWO popadoms at a time and, holding them as one, carefully slip them into the hot oil. As soon as they are immersed, turn them over using tongs or two fish slices. Hold the two popadoms together as one all the time. Allow no more than 2 seconds and remove the popadoms from the hot oil.

Drain on kitchen paper upright (like toast in a toast rack), and not flat, for the best results.

Note: In the restaurant we use a large, aluminium colander for this purpose and put the fried popadoms in side by side. The colander is then placed in a 'hot plate', a piece of equipment rather like the bottom section of a 'hostess' trolley. The technique allows the oil to drain away efficiently and keeps the popadoms warm, dry, and crisp. Placing the cooked popadoms in a warm oven will, of course, be just as effective.

Popadoms may be cooked several hours in advance and warmed just before serving.

ONION SALAD

Served with popadoms together with the yogurt mint sauce.

Preparation time: 5 minutes.

2 onions
1 tomato
½ inch (1cm) piece of cucumber
Generous pinch of salt
Pinch of red chilli powder
1 tsp lemon juice
2 tsp mint sauce (the sort used with roast lamb)

Finely chop the onions, tomato, and cucumber to produce thin strips. Place them in a bowl and add the remaining ingredients. Mix thoroughly.

YOGURT MINT SAUCE

Served with popadoms and a variety of starters.

Preparation time: 5 minutes.

1 UK cup (⅔ US cup/5 fl oz/150ml) plain yogurt
2 tsp mint sauce
½ level tsp salt
¼ tsp chilli powder
¼ tsp garam masala
¼ tsp amchoor
½ level tsp caster (or granulated) sugar
2 drops of green food colouring (optional)

Put all the ingredients into a bowl and mix well.

MINT CHUTNEY

Indian pickles and chutneys can make a good meal absolutely extraordinary. They add a burst of flavour to any meal. Most chutneys and pickles are made from raw, cooked or pickled vegetables and fruits. Serve in small quantities and eat in tiny amounts with each mouthful of food.

Mint chutney does not require any cooking and has a wonderful fresh spicy taste. Tamarind and/or unripe green mango is normally used to add the sweet/sour flavour to this chutney, but using the fruity sauce that I use in this recipe is quick, easy and I think even better.

Chef's tip: Add a handful or more of fresh coriander leaves for a tasty variation.

Makes approximately 1 UK cup (⅔ US cup/5 fl oz/150ml).
Preparation time 10–15 minutes.

2 UK cups (1¼ US cups) (well packed) mint leaves, washed and
   well drained
1 large or 2 small salad onions, peeled and roughly chopped
1–2 green chillies, chopped
1 level tsp salt
¼ tsp garam masala
4 tbsp HP (or similar) fruity sauce

Place everything in a blender or food processor and blend/process until smooth. Keep covered in the fridge for up to a week.

3

THE CURRY SAUCE

This is the most closely guarded of all the secrets of restaurant cooking.

Once prepared, it has a very smooth texture and a pale golden colour. Taste it and it is pleasant with a subtle curry flavour. Every good restaurant has a large pan of the sauce always at hand, with the recipe varying only slightly from chef to chef. It forms the base of all the restaurant curries from the very mild to the very hot and spicy. It will keep in a refrigerator for up to five days, although the best restaurants will prepare no more than three days' requirement in one go. Together with your spices, the prior preparation of the curry sauce, and whatever meat or fish you propose to use, a selection of dishes can be made in a matter of minutes.

You will see that the making of the curry sauce is in fact simple, with no special equipment required other than a blender. It is essential, though, that you follow strictly the instructions for blending and skimming as these are the two procedures that can make the difference between a good curry sauce and a poor one.

The quantities I have given are enough for six to eight people. If you do not require so much, you may halve the quantity of each ingredient, or alternatively freeze the remainder of the finished sauce. I have included freezing instructions where applicable. Although Indian restaurants do not normally do this, it is a perfectly good way of taking advantage of your freezer at home.

HOW TO MAKE THE CURRY SAUCE

For approximately 8 main course dishes.
Preparation and cooking time: about 1½ hours.

2 lb (900g) onions
2 oz (50g) green ginger
2 oz (50g) garlic
2¾ UK pints (3½ US pints/1.57 litres) water
1 tsp salt
1 tin (8 oz/225g) tomatoes
8 tbsp vegetable oil
1 tsp tomato purée
1 tsp turmeric
1 tsp paprika

Stage 1
Peel and rinse the onions, ginger, and garlic. Slice the onions and roughly chop the ginger and garlic.

Put the chopped ginger and garlic into a blender with about 1 to 1½ UK cups (1 US cup/275ml) of the water and blend until smooth.

Take a large saucepan and put into it the onions, the blended garlic and ginger, and the remainder of the water.

Add the salt and bring to the boil. Turn down the heat to very low and simmer, with the lid on, for 40–45 minutes.

Leave to cool.

Stage 2
Once cooled, pour half of the boiled onion mixture into a blender and blend until perfectly smooth. Absolute smoothness is essential. To be certain, blend for at least 2 minutes. Pour the blended onion mixture into a clean pan or bowl and repeat with the other half of the boiled onions.

Wash and dry the saucepan. Reserve about 4 tablespoonfuls of the sauce at this stage to use in cooking the chicken (page 49) and lamb (page 65).

Freezing: Freezing is best done at this stage.

Stage 3

Open the can of tomatoes, pour into the rinsed blender jug, and blend. Again, it is important that they are perfectly smooth, so blend for about 2 minutes.

Into the clean saucepan, put the oil, tomato purée, turmeric, and paprika.

Add the blended tomatoes and bring to the boil. Turn down the heat and cook, stirring occasionally, for 10 minutes.

Now add the onion mixture to the saucepan and bring to the boil again. Turn down the heat enough to keep the sauce at a simmer.

You will notice at this stage that a froth rises to the surface of the sauce. This needs to be skimmed off.

Keep simmering and skimming for 20–25 minutes, stirring now and again to prevent the sauce sticking to the bottom of the saucepan.

Use immediately or cool and refrigerate for up to 4 days.

4

STARTERS AND SIDE DISHES

Menu

TANDOORI CHICKEN – Spring chicken marinated in yogurt, herbs and spices, and cooked at a high heat.

SEEKH KEBABS – Minced lamb with onions, herbs and spices.

NARGIS KEBABS – Hard boiled eggs enclosed in a layer of spicy minced lamb.

RESHMI KEBABS – Succulent pieces of marinated chicken or lamb, lightly spiced and cooked on skewers.

LAMB TIKKA – Marinated lamb pieces cooked quickly at a high heat.

CHICKEN TIKKA – Boneless diced chicken marinated and cooked quickly at a high heat.

ONION BHAJI – Besan (gram flour) flavoured with sliced onion, herbs and spices, and deep fried until crisp on the outside and succulent on the inside.

CHICKEN CHAT – Diced spring chicken in a spicy dressing, served on a crisp green salad.

ALOO CHAT – Diced cooked potatoes, in a spicy dressing, served on a crisp green salad.

TANDOORI FISH – Succulent pieces of fish, marinated and grilled.

TANDOORI KING PRAWNS – Delicately spiced and cooked under a hot grill.

BOMBAY ALOO – Bite sized pieces of cooked potatoes lightly fried with onions, tomatoes and spices.

TANDOORI COOKING

At one time it was believed that dishes cooked in a tandoor could not be satisfactorily reproduced at home using an ordinary convection oven. Whilst it may be true that cooking on charcoal does give it a unique quality, I believe the very high temperatures that are reached in a tandoori oven are more significant than the charcoal that fires it. It is possible to achieve similar conditions at home by heating your oven to the highest possible temperature and cooking the food near the top of the oven where it will be at its hottest.

If you should wish to serve your starters in the same manner as served in Indian restaurants, I have given instructions for sizzling them. A wonderful innovation which gives food a special tantalising allure, it involves buying sizzler dishes. These are heavy, oval cast-iron plates readily available from department stores and suppliers of catering equipment.

HOW TO SIZZLE

Heat the sizzler dish on the hob for about 5 minutes to get it really hot.

Turn off the heat and place some sliced onion onto the dish.

Immediately put the cooked starter on top of the onion and pour 1 tablespoonful of melted vegetable ghee onto the side of the dish. The heat from the dish rapidly heats the fat which, in contact with the onion, starts the sizzling.

Now squirt some lemon juice onto the onions. This produces even more sizzling and a delicious aroma.

Finally, sprinkle with chopped coriander, and serve.

TANDOORI MARINADE

A variety of dishes require that the meat, fish or poultry is marinated prior to cooking. Follow this recipe whenever this is necessary.

Makes 2 UK cups (1¼ US cups).
Preparation time: 5 minutes.

2 UK cups (1¼ US cups/10 fl oz/275ml) plain yogurt
2 green chillies
2 tsp grated green ginger
3 cloves of garlic
1½ tsp salt
1 tsp red chilli powder
1 tsp black cumin
1½ tsp garam masala
2 tsp vinegar
2 tbsp cooking oil
½ tsp red food colouring
½ tsp yellow food colouring

Combine the yogurt, green chillies, ginger, and garlic in a blender until smooth.

Empty into a bowl and add all the remaining ingredients. Beat the mixture until glossy.

TANDOORI CHICKEN

The secret is to buy a chicken no more than 3 lb (1kg 250g) in weight. If you buy portions, ensure that these are from small chickens.

For a main course, double the quantities of everything (including the marinade).

Serves 4 (starters).
Marinating time: 6 hours (or overnight).
Preparation time: 25 minutes.

1 whole chicken or 4 portions
2 UK cups (1¼ US cups/10 fl oz/275ml) tandoori marinade (page 25)

Quarter the chicken if using a whole one, and remove the skin. Make deep slits into the meat right down to the bone, four into each leg portion and two into each breast portion. Wash, and drain well or wipe off excess moisture with kitchen paper.

Now put the chicken into the bowl containing the marinade and mix thoroughly, making sure that the marinade goes into the slits.

Cover and refrigerate for at least 6 hours but preferably overnight. The chicken may be kept in the marinade for up to 3 days without spoiling.

Preheat the oven to its maximum temperature.

Shake off excess marinade from the chicken portions and place on a rack in a shallow baking tray. Bake near the top of the oven for about 20 minutes. Test with a fork to make sure the chicken is cooked – when the flesh will come away from the bone easily.

Serve immediately, sizzling if preferred, with a green salad, lemon wedges, and yogurt mint sauce (page 17).

SEEKH KEBABS

These are made from lean minced lamb that is put through the mincer twice. The meat must be lean to give the correct flavour and texture. Mincing twice enhances the binding of the meat.

Serves 4.
Preparation and cooking time: 30 minutes.

1 egg
1 tbsp chopped onion
1 tbsp chopped green capsicum
2 green chillies
2 tsp fresh ginger, grated
3 cloves of garlic
8 oz (225g) lean minced lamb, minced twice
1 tsp salt
1 tsp garam masala
Pinch of red chilli powder
1 tbsp finely chopped green coriander
1 tsp red food colouring

Blend the egg, onion, capsicum, chillies, ginger, and garlic in an electric blender until smooth.

Pour into a bowl and add all the remaining ingredients and mix thoroughly.

Preheat the oven to its maximum temperature.

Divide the mixture into 8 equal parts, and using floured hands form into sausage shapes about 4 inches (10cm) in length.

Place these on a rack in a shallow baking tray and cook near the top of the oven for 10–12 minutes.

Serve, sizzling if liked, with a green salad, lemon wedges, and yogurt mint sauce (page 17).

NARGIS KEBABS

The Indian version of the Scotch Egg, this dish is becoming increasingly popular. The name Nargis is thought to come from the Persian word for Narcissus, and the Nargis Kebab, or Nargis Kofta as it is sometimes called, has many enthusiasts.

Chef's tip: lightly oil your hands when handling the meat to stop it sticking to your hands.

Serves 4.
Preparation and cooking time: 25–30 minutes.

8 oz (250g) minced lamb
2 cloves of garlic, finely chopped
1 inch (2.5cm) piece of ginger, finely chopped or grated
½ tsp ground coriander
½ tsp ground cumin
½ tsp chilli powder
1 tbsp cornflour
½ tsp salt
1 egg yolk
4 small hard-boiled eggs
2 tbsp oil

Mix together the meat, garlic, ginger, spices, cornflour and salt. Add the egg yolk and mix until well incorporated.

Divide the mixture into 4 equal portions and flatten each portion into a round large enough to enclose the boiled eggs completely.

Place an egg in the centre of each round and bring the meat up to cover the egg. Gently roll into a ball.

Heat the oil in a non-stick pan and shallow fry the kebabs on a medium to high heat until they are brown all over. Turn the heat down a little and continue cooking for 5–6 minutes until the meat is cooked through.

The kebabs can be served covered with an omelette, accompanied by a crisp salad and raita, or in a smooth creamy sauce as a curry (page 75).

RESHMI KEBABS (SILKEN KEBABS)

These smooth as silk kebabs get their name from the succulence of the meat after prolonged marinating and light braising. They can be made with lamb instead of chicken if preferred. Try them with mint chutney (page 18) as a starter, or serve with a dal as a main course.

Serves 4 as a starter, 2–3 as a main course.
Marinating time: 24 hours.
Preparation and cooking time 25–30 minutes.

3 almonds
2–3 green chillies, roughly chopped
3 cloves of garlic, roughly chopped
½ inch (1.25cm) piece of ginger, peeled and chopped
Handful of fresh coriander
1 tsp salt
Juice of ½ lemon
3 tbsp double cream
1 lb (500g) chicken breast fillets, cut into 1 inch (2.5cm) pieces
1 tbsp butter or ghee

Place the almonds in a small bowl and cover with boiling water. Allow to soak for about 5 minutes and slip off the brown skin and chop the almonds roughly.

Place the almonds, chillies, garlic, ginger and coriander into the bowl of a food processor and process until finely chopped.

Transfer the mixture to a non-metallic bowl and add the salt, lemon juice and cream. Add the chicken and mix well to coat. Cover and marinate for 24 hours in the refrigerator.

If using wooden skewers, soak in cold water for about half an hour before using. Also, bring out the chicken from the fridge to bring to room temperature.

Preheat the grill to high and lightly oil the grill pan. Remove the meat from the marinade and thread onto skewers.

Brush with butter or ghee and grill for about 10 minutes, turning once, until cooked through. Serve immediately.

LAMB TIKKA

The meat for this dish must be very lean. From a whole leg of lamb, cut thick succulent strips from the thigh section to reserve for lamb tikka. If you are buying lamb solely for this purpose, you will require approximately 12 oz (350g) of lean meat for 4 people.

Serves 4.
Marinating time: 4–6 hours.
Preparation and cooking time: 30 minutes.

12 oz (350g) lean lamb taken from the leg
1 UK cup (⅔ US cup/5 fl oz/150ml) tandoori marinade (page 25)

Cut the lamb into 16 strips about ¼ inch (0.5cm) thick and 1½ inches (4cm) wide by 2½ inches (6cm) in length (or into 16 equal pieces if this is difficult). Wash the meat and drain, squeezing out excess moisture.

Place the lamb pieces and the marinade in a bowl and mix thoroughly. Cover and refrigerate for 4–6 hours or a maximum of 3 days.

Preheat the oven to its maximum temperature.

Take the lamb pieces out of the bowl and shake off excess marinade. Arrange them on a rack in a large shallow baking tray, in a single layer.

Cook for 15–20 minutes.

Serve immediately, on a sizzler dish if preferred, with a green salad, lemon wedges and yogurt mint sauce (page 17).

Note: If you wish to serve lamb tikka as a main course, double the quantity of meat and marinade.

CHICKEN TIKKA

Delicious tender chunks of chicken are produced following this recipe, lightly spiced but absolutely oozing with flavour.

Serves 4.
Marinating time: 4–6 hours.
Preparation and cooking time: 20 minutes.

3 large chicken fillets
4 tbsp plain yogurt
½ tsp red chilli powder
½ tsp salt
2 tsp cooking oil
Pinch of yellow food colouring

Cut each chicken fillet into 6 equal-sized chunks. Wash and drain them.

Place all the remaining ingredients into a bowl and mix well.

Add the chicken pieces to the bowl and mix again, making sure that all the pieces are well coated with the yogurt.

Cover and refrigerate for 4–6 hours or a maximum of 3 days.

Preheat the oven to its maximum temperature.

Place the chicken pieces onto a rack in a shallow baking tray in a single layer.

Bake near the top of the oven for 10 minutes or until cooked through.

Serve immediately, sizzling if preferred, with a green salad, wedges of lemon and yogurt mint sauce (page 17).

ONION BHAJI

A popular starter amongst vegetarians and meat eaters alike, onion bhajis can also be served as a teatime snack.

Serves 4.
Preparation and cooking time: 15 minutes.

4 medium-sized onions
8 oz (225g) gram flour
4 level tsp salt
2 tbsp mint sauce
1 tsp garam masala
1 tsp finely chopped green coriander
Oil for deep frying

Peel, wash, and thinly slice the onions.

Sift the gram flour and salt into a bowl and add enough cold water to make a stiff batter.

Add the onions and all the remaining ingredients to the batter and mix well.

Heat the oil in a frying pan, then drop tablespoonfuls of the mixture into the hot oil and fry for about 3 minutes.

Remove the bhajis from the oil and press into circular flat patti shapes.

Return to the oil and cook for a further 2–3 minutes until the outside is dark brown.

Serve with a green salad and yogurt mint sauce (page 17).

CHICKEN CHAT

Chicken that has been prepared using the method for the preparation of chicken for curries (page 49) is ideal for this tangy refreshing starter. However, if you are not planning to make any of the curry dishes that require this particular method of preparation, you may cook the chicken using any of the following methods.

Microwave

Wash the chicken fillets and cut each one into 8 equal-sized pieces. Toss the chicken in 1 tablespoonful of oil to which has been added ½ teaspoonful of salt, a pinch of turmeric, and a pinch of garam masala. Microwave on high for 4–5 minutes, according to the instructions on your microwave, stirring every minute. Allow the chicken to cool completely before proceeding with the recipe.

Saucepan

Wash and cut the chicken pieces as described above. Put 3 tablespoonfuls of oil, ½ teaspoonful of salt, a pinch of turmeric, and a pinch of garam masala into a saucepan. Heat the oil for a few seconds until the spices begin to froth, and add the chicken. Stir and cook covered on a low heat for 10–15 minutes, or until the chicken is cooked, stirring occasionally. Drain off the oil and allow the chicken to cool completely before making into chat.

Serves 4.
Preparation time: 10 minutes.

2 chicken fillets, cooked as suggested
1 tsp French mustard
2 tbsp olive oil
1 tsp chat masala
2 tbsp lemon juice
¼ tsp salt
¼ tsp garam masala
1 tsp finely chopped green coriander

To serve: **lettuce, tomato, and cucumber**

Cut each chunk of chicken again into 4 pieces and put into a bowl.

Place all the remaining ingredients into a screw-top jar and shake to mix. Alternatively, put them into a bowl and beat with a spoon.

Pour the dressing over the chicken, stir gently, and divide into 4 portions.

Serve on a bed of shredded lettuce, garnished with sliced tomato and cucumber.

ALOO CHAT

This is a cool refreshing starter suitable for vegetarians.

Serves 4.
Preparation and cooking time: 35 minutes.

2 medium-sized potatoes
1 tsp French mustard
2 tbsp olive oil
1 tsp chat masala
2 tbsp lemon juice
¼ tsp salt
¼ tsp garam masala
1 tsp finely chopped green coriander

To serve: **lettuce, tomato, and cucumber**

Cook the potatoes, in their jackets, in boiling salted water until soft. Drain and allow to cool.

Meanwhile, put all the remaining ingredients into a screw-top jar and shake well to mix, or put them into a bowl and beat with a fork until well mixed.

Peel the potatoes and cut into ½ inch (1cm) dice. Place them in a bowl and pour the dressing over them.

Divide into 4 portions and serve on a bed of shredded lettuce, garnished with sliced tomato and cucumber.

TANDOORI FISH

We use cod for this but you may use any white fish that you prefer, such as skate or whiting. Ask the fishmonger to remove all the skin, including the white skin.

Serves 4.
Marinating time: 4–6 hours.
Preparation and cooking time: 15 minutes.

12 oz (350g) skinned white fish
1 UK cup (⅔ US cup/5 fl oz/150ml) tandoori marinade (page 25)

Wash the fish and cut into equal-sized chunks, about 1 inch (2.5cm) square.

Put the marinade in a bowl and immerse the fish pieces in it, ensuring that all of them become coated with the marinade.

Cover and refrigerate for 4–6 hours or a maximum of 24 hours.

Preheat the oven to its maximum temperature.

Remove the fish pieces from the marinade, shaking off any excess. Place them on a rack in a shallow baking tray in a single layer.

Bake near the top of the oven for 7–8 minutes.

Serve immediately with a green salad, lemon wedges and yogurt mint sauce (page 17).

Note: Instead of baking you may grill the fish pieces under a hot grill, without turning, for 6–7 minutes.

TANDOORI KING PRAWNS

In the UK we always buy frozen uncooked prawns still in their shells for this mouth-watering starter. If you can get fresh prawns, that would be ideal. Ready cooked prawns are not suitable.

Serves 4.
Preparation and cooking time: 15 minutes.

16 king prawns
1 UK cup (⅔ US cup/5 fl oz/150ml) tandoori marinade (page 25)

Remove shells and beards from the prawns, wash and drain.

In a bowl, mix together the prawns and the marinade, making sure that the prawns are well coated.

There is no need to marinate these for long and in fact they should not be left for longer than a few minutes.

Preheat the oven to its maximum temperature.

Remove the prawns from the marinade, shaking off excess, and place on a rack in a shallow baking tray.

Bake near the top of the oven for 7–8 minutes.

Serve, sizzling on a sizzler dish if liked, with a green salad, lemon slices and yogurt mint sauce (page 17).

Note: Instead of baking, the prawns may be grilled under a very hot grill for about 5 minutes, turning once.

Allow appropriately increased quantities if you wish to serve tandoori prawns as a main course dish.

BOMBAY ALOO

This spicy potato dish is excellent served as a side dish. Or try it with poppadoms and yogurt mint sauce as a snack – delicious.

Serves 4.
Preparation and cooking time: 40–45 minutes.

3 potatoes, peeled and chopped into bite-size pieces
2 tsp salt
1 tsp turmeric
6 tbsp oil
½ onion, finely chopped
2 inch (5cm) piece ginger, grated
4 cloves of garlic, sliced
1 tsp garam masala
1 tsp cumin powder
1 tsp chilli powder
½ tsp salt
½ onion, sliced
½ green capsicum, sliced
2 tbsp tomato purée
1 tbsp lemon juice
1 tomato, cut into 8 pieces
4 tbsp chopped coriander

Boil the potatoes in water with a little salt and turmeric added until cooked.

Meanwhile, heat the oil in a karahi or deep frying pan, and fry the finely chopped onion for about 3 minutes, until translucent.

Add the ginger, garlic, garam masala, cumin and chilli powder, and stir fry for 2 minutes.

Add the half teaspoonful of salt, the sliced onion, capsicum, tomato purée, lemon juice and tomato, and stir fry for 2 minutes.

Drain the potatoes and add to the pan. Mix well and serve immediately, sprinkled with the coriander.

5

BREADS

Menu

NAN – A flat leavened bread that is light and soft with a slightly crisp exterior.

KEEMA NAN – A nan bread with spiced minced lamb spread onto one surface.

ONION KULCHA – A nan bread to which onion and spices have been added. Masala kulcha is a similar one with vegetables.

BHATURA – Very soft, round breads made with yogurt dough that is deep fried.

CHAPATTI – A round flat leavened bread made with wholemeal or wheatmeal flour.

PARATHA – A square, flat leavened bread made with a wholemeal or wheatmeal dough that is layered with butter.

Opposite are some of the many kinds of bread served in Indian restaurants, and there are many more kinds which are not. Although the nan breads are the most familiar and perhaps the most popular, I have included recipes for a few others which are very good eaten with Indian curries, bhajis, and yogurts. In some instances they are also easier to make at home, with a little practice.

A variety of flours are used to make such breads, ranging from those flours made from various grains to those made by grinding pulses.

For my recipes you will require only two kinds of flour.

One is ordinary white flour. The other is a finely ground wholemeal flour called atta or chapatti flour. This is often sold in large bags, but if you can get it in the quantities you want, by all means buy it. If not, buy wholemeal flour and mix it with about 1 cup of plain white flour to 3 cups of the wholemeal. This gives the dough the softness and pliability required for our breads.

EQUIPMENT AND UTENSILS

Breads such as nans are best made in a tandoor which is the name given to a clay oven. At home, a very heavy baking tray, a very hot oven and a hot grill will give good results.

Some of our breads, such as the bhatura, are deep fried. The best utensil for deep frying is the karahi, a utensil similar to the Chinese wok but deeper and more rounded. A chip pan or deep frying pan will suffice if you do not own a karahi.

Breads such as chapattis and parathas are cooked on tavas. These are slightly concave, cast-iron plates, and the nearest thing to them would be a heavy cast-iron frying pan.

QUICK NAN RECIPE

Although I refer to this as a quick recipe it is by no means a short cut, but a recipe without yeast which, of course, eliminates the time required for proving. Even so, this recipe produces wonderfully light, fluffy nan breads which are best eaten immediately.

Makes 6 nans.
Preparation and cooking time: about 30 minutes.

1 lb (450g) self-raising flour, plus extra for dusting
½ tsp salt
½ tsp baking powder
2 tbsp vegetable oil
4 tbsp plain yogurt, beaten
2 eggs, beaten
1 UK cup (⅔ US cup/5 fl oz/150ml) water (approximately)
A little melted vegetable ghee

Sift the flour, salt, and baking powder into a bowl. Add the oil, yogurt, and eggs and mix in with a fork.

Now add the water little by little and, using your hands, bring the flour together to make a soft dough.

Knead the dough with damp hands for a minute or two until it is smooth; cover it and leave to rest for at least 15 minutes.

Meanwhile, preheat the oven to its highest temperature. Put a heavy baking tray to heat in the oven, and preheat your grill.

Divide the dough into 6 equal portions. Dust your hands and taking one portion, roll it into a ball in the palms of your hands.

Roll the ball out into a tear shape, or a round if you prefer.

Carefully take the hot baking tray out of the oven, slap the nan onto it and immediately return to the oven for about 3 minutes.

Remove the baking tray and the nan from the oven and place them under a hot grill for 30 seconds to brown lightly and crisp the top.

Brush the top with the melted ghee and wrap in a clean napkin or tea towel and keep warm.

Repeat the process with all of the remaining dough. Make two nans at a time if the size of your baking tray and grill will permit.

Serve immediately.

YEAST NAN RECIPE

This yeast recipe also produces a delicious nan. It requires a little more time than the quick nan recipe but the breads are more suitable for reheating.

Makes 6 nans.
Preparation and cooking time: 30 minutes, plus an hour to prove the dough.

1 UK cup (⅔ US cup/5 fl oz/150ml) milk (hand hot)
2 tbsp caster sugar
1 tbsp instant dried yeast
1 lb (450g) plain flour, plus extra for dusting
½ tsp salt
1 tsp baking powder
2 tbsp vegetable oil
5 fl oz (150ml) plain yogurt, beaten
1 large egg, beaten
A little melted vegetable ghee

Pour the milk into a bowl and stir in the sugar and the yeast. Set aside for 15 minutes until the mixture is frothy.

Sift the flour, salt, and baking powder into another bowl. Add to it the yeast mixture and all the remaining ingredients (except the ghee), and mix into a dough.

Place the dough onto a clean surface and knead it for 10 minutes or so, until it is smooth.

Put the dough in a greased bowl, cover with greased cling film, and set aside in a warm place for about an hour. The dough will double in size.

Knead the dough again lightly before proceeding to make the nans as described in the previous recipe.

KEEMA NAN

These require a little of the mixture for seekh kebabs (page 27) to be spread thinly on the surface of each nan before placing in the oven.

ONION KULCHA

Here, thinly sliced onions are pressed into the nans before baking.

For 6 kulchas, thinly slice 2 onions, sprinkle them with salt, and leave to stand for about an hour.

Drain off the liquid and pat dry with kitchen paper. Mix a teaspoonful of garam masala and 2 teaspoonfuls of finely chopped coriander with the onions and use by pressing onto the surface of each nan before cooking.

MASALA KULCHA

For these, a mixture of cooked vegetables is pressed onto the surface of each nan before cooking. Cooked vegetables such as potatoes, peas and onions are ideal. Just mix with a little salt and garam masala and they are ready for use.

BHATURAS

These deliciously soft breads are not normally served in Indian restaurants. I include them because they are ideal cooked in advance and reheated and also because they are probably the easiest of all the Indian breads to make.

Makes 8–10.
Preparation and cooking time: 30 minutes.

8 oz (225g) white or chapatti flour
½ tsp baking powder
½ tsp salt
1½ UK cups (1 US cup/220ml) plain yogurt (approximately)
Oil for deep frying

Sift the flour, baking powder, and salt into a bowl.

Slowly add the yogurt and gather the flour together with your fingertips until you have a soft dough.

Knead lightly and set aside to rest for at least 15 minutes.

Heat the oil in a deep pan or karahi on a medium heat. Meanwhile, divide the dough into 8 portions without rolling into balls.

Dust your hands with flour and take one of the portions of dough and form into a ball.

Flatten the ball, dust well, and roll out into a 7–8 inch (17–20cm) round.

Now turn up the heat under the oil for a minute or two to get it really hot.

Slide the bhatura carefully into the hot oil. It will sink at first but, if the oil is hot enough, it will rise to the surface in seconds.

Using a slotted spoon, push it back into the oil briefly and then turn it over for a few seconds.

Remove the bhatura from the oil with the slotted spoon and put it on a plate lined with kitchen paper.

Repeat with the remaining dough. Drain the bhaturas well on kitchen paper and either serve immediately or wrap in foil for reheating later.

Tip: If you are making just a few bhaturas, you may like to roll them all out before frying them.

CHAPATTIS

These flat, round breads are made with atta (sometimes called chapatti flour). Three parts wholemeal flour with one part plain white flour may be used instead. Mix it with water to a soft, slightly sticky dough and leave to rest at least 15 minutes before using.

Chapattis are cooked on a tava, that is a circular cast-iron plate with a long handle. A heavy cast-iron frying pan would make a suitable substitute.

Practice makes perfect when it comes to chapatti making, so do not be put off if your first efforts are not as good as you would like. They will taste fine even if they do not look immaculate.

Makes 8–10.
Preparation and cooking time: about 30 minutes.

8 oz (225g) chapatti flour, with extra for dusting
Just under 1 UK cup (⅔ US cup/110ml) water (very approximately)

Put the flour into a bowl. Add the water a little at a time and bring the flour together with the fingertips.

As the dough becomes stickier, draw it together with your hands, adding more water until all the flour is incorporated and you have a soft, pliable dough.

Knead the dough with wet hands for a minute or two. Fold into a neat shape, dampen the surface, cover and leave to rest for 15 minutes.

Put the tava on the hob to preheat on a medium heat.

Roughly divide the dough into 8–10 parts without forming into balls.

Now dust your hands lightly with the extra flour and take a portion of the dough. Roll it between your hands into a ball. If it feels sticky, use a little extra flour on your hands.

Put the ball of dough into the flour and press flat, dusting on both sides.

Roll out into a round about 6 inches (15cm) in diameter, dusting when required.

Pick up the chapatti, pat between your hands for a few seconds to shake off excess flour, and slap it onto the hot tava.

Let it cook for about 30 seconds and turn it over. (If the chapatti sticks to the tava, it is not hot enough. If the markings on the chapatti are too dark, it is too hot. Adjust as necessary.)

Cook for about 30 seconds on the second side, lifting the chapatti off the tava and replacing it immediately half way through.

Turn over again, now lift the chapatti off the tava and place it directly over a medium flame, moving it about all the time. It will puff up in seconds.

Place the chapatti in a clean napkin, folding over the top to keep warm.

Repeat with the remaining dough. Stack the chapattis in the napkin as you make them.

Ideally, chapattis should be eaten immediately, but if you wish to keep them for later, wrap them in aluminium foil and keep them in a refrigerator. Place, still in foil, in a hot oven for about 20 minutes to reheat. Alternatively reheat in a microwave oven without the foil.

Freezing: Chapattis freeze well. Stack and wrap in foil and freeze for up to a month. They may be thawed and reheated without removing the foil.

PARATHAS

These are made with the same flour as chapattis but are layered with ghee before being cooked on the tava with more ghee brushed onto them. Vegetable oil is sometimes used instead of ghee and this is perfectly acceptable although I feel that the ghee produces the best flavour. Alternatively, you may use butter. This, because of the water content in butter, results in a softer, less crisp paratha which I love. It really is a matter of personal preference and convenience which you use, and you may like to try all three before making up your mind.

Makes 6–8.
Preparation and cooking time: about 30 minutes.

8 oz (225g) chapatti flour, plus extra for dusting
Just under 1 UK cup (⅔ US cup/110ml) water (approximately)
6 tbsp melted ghee

Make the dough as for chapattis (page 44) and leave to rest for 15–30 minutes.

Put the tava or cast-iron frying pan onto a medium heat. Meanwhile, divide the dough into 6–8 equal portions.

Take one portion with floured hands and roll into a ball.

Place the ball of dough into the flour and press flat, dusting on both sides.

Roll out into a 6 inch (15cm) round, and brush the surface with melted ghee.

Now fold by taking opposite sides and folding until they meet in the middle. You should have a long rectangular shape.

Brush the top surface again with melted ghee and fold, this time bringing in the ends of the rectangle to meet in the middle.

Brush the dry surface for the final time with melted ghee and fold into half. You should have a square.

Place this in the flour, press flat, and roll out into an 8 inch (20cm) square.

Pat between your hands and slap onto the hot tava. Cook for about 30 seconds whilst brushing the top surface with ghee. Turn over.

Again brush the surface uppermost with the ghee and turn over, having given the second side 30 seconds.

Continue to cook the first side for a further 30 seconds whilst brushing more melted ghee on the top surface.

Turn over for the final time and cook for a further few seconds.

Both sides should have reddish brown spots. The frequent turning over ensures even cooking.

Put the paratha on a plate lined with a large piece of aluminium foil. Fold over the foil to keep the paratha warm while you make all the parathas in this way.

Like chapattis, parathas are best eaten immediately but are quite good reheated.

6

CHICKEN DISHES

Menu

CHICKEN CURRY – Mild, Madras or vindaloo.

CHICKEN BHUNA MASALA – Boneless chicken cooked in spices and flavoured with green herbs.

CHICKEN MUGHLAI – Chicken pieces cooked with fruits, egg, and herbs in a cream sauce.

CHICKEN DOPIAZA – Mildly spiced chicken cooked with onions.

CHICKEN KORMA – Chicken cooked with cream and nuts, mildly spiced.

CHICKEN DHANSAK – Chicken and lentils cooked in spices.

CHICKEN SAGWALA – Chicken and spinach cooked in spices.

CHICKEN TIKKA MASALA – Boneless chicken, marinated and cooked, blended in a delicate creamy sauce with herbs and spices.

MAKHAN CHICKEN – Tandoori chicken in a delectable cream sauce.

CHICKEN JALFREZI – Moist chicken pieces with tomato, onion and capsicum in a spicy, dry sauce.

CHICKEN STUFFED CHILLI PEPPER – Mild, peppery banana chillies, stuffed with minced spiced chicken and potato, coated in a crispy batter and deep fried.

The Right Equipment

A restaurant chef always uses a large frying pan with deep sides (approximately 4 inches or 10cm) for cooking his curries. This is important and results in a large amount of food being in contact with the hot surface at one time and a large area for the evaporation of water. Not only does this speed up cooking, but it allows a more rapid thickening of the sauces without overcooking the meat, fish, or vegetables. If you do not have such a pan already, it is well worth investing in one. Alternatively, use a saucepan large enough to afford you the same benefits.

How to Prepare the Chicken

This is the basic method of preparation which is common to most recipes in this chapter.

For our curries we have always used only breast portions of chicken cooked in a special way. Some restaurants use the whole chicken, but their methods of boiling and removing the flesh from the bones can leave an unwanted boiled taste and some less savoury bits of meat in the finished dish. I would strongly recommend that you follow my suggestion as the end result is well worth it, and you will be amazed how tender the chicken turns out to be.

Preparation and cooking time: 25 minutes.
For 6–8 people you will require:

5 large chicken breasts (approximately 2 lb/900g with skin and bone removed)
6 tbsp vegetable oil
1 tsp turmeric
4 tbsp reserved curry sauce, prepared to the end of stage 2 (page 20)

With a sharp knife remove all fat and membranes from the chicken portions and cut each into 8 equal-sized pieces. Wash and drain.

Place the oil, turmeric and curry sauce into a large saucepan and mix well.

Cook on a medium heat, stirring continuously until the sauce starts to darken in colour (approximately 4–5 minutes).

Add the chicken and stir until all the pieces are well coated with the sauce.

Turn down the heat and continue cooking with the lid on for 15–20 minutes, or until the chicken is tender, stirring frequently.

Remove the chicken pieces (leaving behind the sediment) and place them in a clean container. The cooked chicken can now be used immediately for many of the chicken curries or cooled and refrigerated for up to 4 days.

Freezing: Freeze for up to 2 months.

How to Make the Curries

Making the curries once you have the sauce is extremely easy. However, read this page carefully as there are a few points that you will find helpful.

In all the following recipes I have allowed for 3–4 servings. If you have frozen half of the sauce and meat after following my recipes on pages 20 and 49, your next Indian meal will be as quick and simple as going to your favourite restaurant, and just as delicious. If you wish to cater for twice this number, then using the full quantity of sauce will permit you to make two different main dishes, or one main dish and two vegetable, or side dishes as they are known in Indian restaurants. You could, of course, make an even greater variety of dishes if you want, bearing in mind that my recipe for curry sauce is enough for up to eight main course dishes.

You may feel that the amount of oil in my recipes seems large. If this is the case, do not be tempted to reduce it at the cooking stage, but instead skim off the top of the finished curry. A generous quantity of oil is essential to bring out the flavour of the spices, and create the right texture in the sauce.

One more point, and that is about food colourings. Indian restaurants use liberal amounts of red and yellow food colourings. While these are not important to the actual flavour of the food, they make an enormous difference to its appearance. Also, the public is used to particular dishes being a certain colour, and some people are not pleased if their favourite dish is not the colour they expected. I recall an incident when a couple walked out of our restaurant because the colour of their chicken tikka was not the deep red they were used to. Yet they had not eaten a morsel of it! Had they done so, they would have found it to be excellent as it is one dish we are particularly proud of, and our customers would certainly agree! However, if you are not happy using artificial colourings you may use natural ones available from healthfood stores, or omit them altogether.

We tend to use the minimum amount of food colourings, but some dishes (and some people as I have explained) demand them – for instance tandoori chicken would not, I am sure, be acceptable if it were any colour other than red. Chicken tikka masala is another dish that is expected to be a distinctive colour. For these reasons I have included colourings in my recipes where we would normally use them, but if you were really against them a little extra paprika and/or turmeric produces good results.

CHICKEN CURRY

This is a basic curry dish which is simple to make, requiring little other than the cooked chicken and the curry sauce. If you wish to make this into a chicken Madras, use 1 teaspoonful of chilli powder. Double this amount if you want a vindaloo.

Serves 3–4.
Preparation and cooking time: about 15 minutes.

5 tbsp vegetable oil
3 UK cups (2 US cups/15 fl oz/425ml) curry sauce (page 20)
1 tsp salt
Pinch of chilli powder
1 lb (450g) chicken cooked as on page 49
1 level tsp garam masala
½ level tsp ground cumin
Pinch of dried fenugreek leaves, ground
½ tomato, thinly sliced
1 tbsp finely chopped green coriander

Heat the oil in a large, deep frying pan, and add the curry sauce, and bring to the boil.

Without reducing the heat, add the salt, chilli powder and chicken, and continue cooking for about 5 minutes.

Now turn down the heat and stir in the garam masala, ground cumin and fenugreek. Simmer for a further 2–3 minutes.

Put in the sliced tomato and half the coriander and cook for another 2 minutes. Skim off any excess oil and serve sprinkled with the remaining coriander.

A little trick. During the last couple of minutes of cooking, a restaurant chef will often stir in a teaspoonful or so of the marinade used for tandoori chicken. This improves the texture and flavour of the sauce as well as improving the colour.

CHICKEN BHUNA MASALA

This spicy dish is a firm favourite. Remember, spicy does not necessarily mean hot!

Serves 3–4.
Preparation and cooking time: 15–20 minutes.

2 oz (50g) mushrooms
½ green capsicum
6 tbsp vegetable oil
3 UK cups (2 US cups/15 fl oz/425ml) curry sauce (page 20)
1 lb (450g) chicken, cooked as on page 49
1 tsp salt
½ tsp chilli powder
1 green chilli, finely chopped
½ tsp red food colouring
1½ tsp garam masala
1 tsp ground cumin
½ tsp dried fenugreek leaves, ground
1 tbsp finely chopped green coriander

Wash the mushrooms and capsicum and slice thinly. Heat the oil in a large, deep frying pan, add the sliced vegetables, and fry for 4–5 minutes on a medium heat.

Add the curry sauce, chicken, salt, chilli powder and green chilli, and food colouring. Turn up the heat and bring to the boil. Continue cooking for 5 minutes, stirring frequently.

Turn down the heat slightly and stir in the garam masala, ground cumin and fenugreek, and cook for a further 5 minutes, stirring now and again.

Spoon off any excess oil and serve sprinkled with green coriander.

CHICKEN MUGHLAI

This is another dish suitable for those who do not like their curries spicy. It has a creamy sauce with egg added to it for more body.

Serves 4.
Preparation and cooking time: 15–20 minutes.

6 tbsp vegetable oil
3 UK cups (2 US cups/15 fl oz/425ml) curry sauce (page 20)
1 lb (450g) chicken, cooked as on page 49
1 tsp salt
¼ tsp yellow food colouring
2 eggs
5 fl oz (150ml) single cream
1½ tsp garam masala
1 tsp ground cumin
4 mango slices, tinned or fresh
1 tbsp finely chopped green coriander

Heat the oil in a large, deep frying pan. Add the curry sauce and bring to the boil on a high heat.

Add the chicken, salt, and food colouring. Stir well and continue cooking on a high heat for about 5 minutes, stirring regularly.

Now turn down the heat to medium and simmer for a further 5 minutes, stirring occasionally.

Meanwhile, whisk the eggs and combine with the cream. Spoon off any excess oil that will have risen to the surface, and stir in the egg and cream mixture.

Also stir in the garam masala and ground cumin. Continue cooking for a further 2–3 minutes, stirring more or less continuously.

Serve garnished with mango slices and green coriander.

CHICKEN DOPIAZA

This is a mildly spiced dish cooked with onions. A delicious variation on the basic chicken curry.

Serves 3–4.
Preparation and cooking time: 15 minutes.

6 tbsp vegetable oil
2 small onions, peeled and sliced into rings
3 UK cups (2 US cups/15 fl oz/425ml) curry sauce (page 20)
1 tsp salt
1 level tsp chilli powder
1 lb (450g) chicken, cooked as on page 49
1 level tsp garam masala
1 level tsp ground cumin
½ level tsp ground coriander
½ level tsp dried fenugreek leaves, ground
1 tbsp finely chopped green coriander

Heat the oil in a large, deep frying pan. Add the sliced onions and fry until transparent but not starting to brown. Add the curry sauce, mix well, and bring to a simmer. Stir in the salt, chilli powder, and chicken. Cook on a medium heat for 10 minutes or until the sauce is quite thick, stirring occasionally.

Now stir in the garam masala, cumin, ground coriander and fenugreek. Continue simmering for 3–4 minutes.

Skim off any excess oil and serve sprinkled with the coriander.

CHICKEN KORMA

This dish is a deliciously creamy one preferred by those who like their curries mild.

Serves 3–4.
Preparation and cooking time: 15 minutes.

4 tbsp vegetable oil
3 UK cups (2 US cups/15 fl oz/425ml) curry sauce (page 20)
1 lb (450g) chicken, cooked as on page 49
2 tbsp cashew nuts, finely chopped
1½ tsp salt
¼ tsp yellow food colouring
½ tsp garam masala
1 tsp ground cumin
5 fl oz (150ml) single cream
2 tsp finely chopped green coriander

Heat the oil in a large, deep frying pan and add to it the curry sauce. Bring to the boil on a high heat.

Do not reduce the heat. Add the chicken, cashew nuts, salt and food colouring. Stir, and cook for 5 minutes or so, stirring regularly.

Turn down the heat slightly and continue to cook for a further 5 minutes. Stir in the garam masala and ground cumin.

Now stir in the cream and heat gently for 3–4 minutes, stirring all the time.

Serve sprinkled with the green coriander.

CHICKEN DHANSAK

This variation combines chicken with lentil dal. It requires less curry sauce because of this and is a tasty dish for those who like the flavour of lentils. This is a hot, sour dish to which you could also add pineapple chunks if you wish.

Serves 3–4.
Preparation and cooking time: 15–20 minutes.

6 tbsp vegetable oil
2 UK cups (1¼ US cups/10 fl oz/275ml) curry sauce (page 20)
2 UK cups (1¼ US cups) of lentil dal (page 94)
1 lb (450g) chicken, cooked as on page 49
½ tsp salt
½ tsp chilli powder
1 green chilli, finely chopped
1½ tsp garam masala
1 tsp ground cumin
2 tbsp lemon juice
1 tbsp finely chopped green coriander

Heat the oil in a large, deep frying pan, add the curry sauce and lentils and bring to the boil.

Without turning down the heat, add the chicken, salt, chilli powder and green chilli.

Stir well and continue to cook on a high heat for about 5 minutes, or until the sauce thickens, stirring regularly.

Now turn down the heat to a simmer for a further 5 minutes. Stir occasionally.

Skim off any excess oil and stir in the garam masala, ground cumin, and lemon juice.

Serve sprinkled with the green coriander.

CHICKEN SAGWALA

This is an unusual but tasty combination of chicken and spinach.

Serves 4.
Preparation and cooking time: 20–25 minutes.

6 tbsp oil
3 UK cups (2 US cups/15 fl oz/425ml) curry sauce (page 20)
16 oz (450g) can puréed spinach
1 tsp salt
1 tsp chilli powder
1 green chilli, finely chopped (optional)
1 lb (450g) chicken, cooked as on page 49
1½ tsp garam masala
2 tsp finely chopped green coriander

Heat the oil in a large, deep frying pan, add the curry sauce and spinach, stir, and bring to the boil.

Stir in the salt, chilli powder and green chilli, and continue to cook until the mixture becomes quite thick. This takes about 10–15 minutes and the oil should start to separate when this is right. Stir frequently and ensure that it does not stick to the pan.

Now add the chicken and the garam masala and simmer on a very low heat for a further 5 minutes, stirring now and again.

Take off the heat, stir in the coriander, and serve.

CHICKEN TIKKA MASALA

A delicious, slightly creamy, medium spiced dish made with chicken tikka.

Serves 3–4.
Preparation and cooking time: 15 minutes.

4 tbsp vegetable oil
3 UK cups (2 US cups/15 fl oz/425ml) curry sauce (page 20)
1 tsp paprika
1 tsp salt
1 level tsp chilli powder
Pinch of red food colouring
1 tsp garam masala
½ tsp ground cumin
3 chicken fillets, freshly made into chicken tikka (page 31)
6 tbsp single cream
1 tbsp finely chopped green coriander

Heat the oil in a large, deep frying pan, add the curry sauce, and bring to the boil.

Without reducing the heat, add the paprika, salt, chilli powder and food colouring. Cook for 5 minutes, stirring frequently, or until the sauce thickens.

Turn down the heat and add the garam masala and cumin powder. Stir. Cook for 3 minutes.

Cut each piece of chicken tikka into two smaller pieces, stir them, with the cream, into the sauce and simmer for a further 2–3 minutes.

Serve sprinkled with the coriander.

MAKHAN CHICKEN

This is a fairly simple but quite spectacular dish in which tandoori chicken (page 26) is transformed by a delectable creamy sauce.

Serves 3–4.
Preparation and cooking time: 30 minutes.

2 oz (50g) butter, preferably unsalted
2 UK cups (1¼ US cups/10 fl oz/275ml) curry sauce (page 20)
2 tbsp tomato purée
1 level tsp garam masala
½ tsp salt
½ tsp ground cumin
1 green chilli, finely chopped
1 tbsp finely chopped green coriander
3 tsp lemon juice
2 UK cups (1¼ US cups/10 fl oz/275ml) single cream
4 portions freshly cooked tandoori chicken

Melt the butter in a large, deep frying pan. Add the curry sauce, tomato purée, garam masala, salt, cumin, chilli, coriander and lemon juice. Mix well.

Bring to a simmer and cook on a medium heat for a minute or so, mixing in the butter as you do so.

Stir in the cream, cook for another minute, and add the chicken pieces.

Stir once and serve.

CHICKEN JALFREZI

With a fresh taste of capsicums and tomatoes, this delicious curry has a really thick sauce that clings to the meat and vegetables.

Serves 4.
Marinating time: 2–3 hours (or overnight).
Preparation and cooking time: 30–35 minutes.

1 lb (500g) chicken breast fillets
1 tsp turmeric
1 tsp of grated ginger
2 tsp of garam masala
1 tsp salt
½ tsp red chilli powder
4 tbsp vegetable oil
2 medium onions, cut into 1 inch (2.5cm) pieces
2 medium green capsicum, de-seeded and cut into 1 inch (2.5cm) pieces
3–4 medium ripe tomatoes, cut into wedges
1 tbsp tomato paste
1 or more green chillies according to taste, chopped
1 UK cup (⅔ US cup/5 fl oz/150ml) curry sauce (page 20)
Chopped fresh coriander leaves for garnish

Wash the chicken and wipe dry with paper towels. Slice each fillet into 5–6 pieces of roughly equal size.

In a medium-sized non-metallic bowl, mix the turmeric, grated ginger, garam masala, salt, chilli powder and 1 tablespoonful of the oil. Add the chicken and mix well. Cover with plastic film or a lid and place in the fridge to marinate for 2–3 hours or overnight. Remember to remove from the fridge about 30 minutes before cooking to allow the chicken to return to room temperature.

Heat 2 tablespoonfuls of the oil in a large deep frying pan or karahi over a high heat. Add the onion and capsicum pieces and fry for 3–4 minutes, stirring constantly until the vegetables start to look opaque. They shouldn't colour.

Turn down the heat a little, add the tomatoes and stir fry for a minute or so. Turn down the heat and transfer the vegetables to a clean bowl and set aside.

Place the pan on the heat again and add the remaining oil. When hot, stir in the marinated chicken and stir fry for about 5 minutes. Add the tomato paste and chopped chillies and fry for another minute.

Now add the curry sauce and continue to cook on a medium heat, stirring until much of the moisture has evaporated from the sauce and the chicken is well cooked (about 5 minutes).

Add the fried vegetables to the pan with the chicken and stir through. Cook on medium heat for another 3–4 minutes. Serve sprinkled with fresh coriander.

CHICKEN STUFFED CHILLI PEPPER

Spicy chicken stuffed in a peppery banana chilli and fried until golden and crisp. Banana chillies are yellowish-green mild-tasting chillies, the shape of a banana and about half the size.

Chef's tip: If you are keeping the chillies and batter for final frying the next day, add another dessertspoonful of besan flour to the batter to freshen and thicken it as it will have become a little runnier on standing.

Serves 4.
Preparation and cooking time: 30–35 minutes.

8 oz (250g) chicken mince
1 tbsp oil
1 tsp salt
½ tsp red chilli powder
1 tsp coriander powder
½ tsp cumin powder
Juice of ½ a lemon
2 heaped tbsp cooked rice or mashed potato
2 tbsp chopped coriander leaves
8 banana chillies
6 tbsp besan flour
2 tbsp rice flour
¼ tsp baking soda
Oil for deep frying

Mix the chicken with the oil, half a teaspoonful of salt, the chilli powder, coriander powder, cumin powder and lemon juice. Cook in a hot pan for 3–4 minutes, stirring constantly. Transfer to a medium-sized bowl and leave to cool slightly. Add the cooked rice or mashed potato and coriander leaves.

Wash the chillies and wipe dry. Slit each chilli along its length, leaving about half an inch (1cm) each end intact. Carefully open up the chilli and remove the seeds and ribs – using a teaspoon makes this easier.

Using small portions at a time, stuff the chillies with the chicken mixture, taking care not to rip the flesh.

Mix the besan flour, rice flour, the remaining half a teaspoonful of salt and the baking soda in a medium bowl. Add enough cold water to make a coating batter, about the consistency of single cream.

Heat some oil in a karahi or deep pan until moderately hot (when the surface of the oil starts to shimmer). Dip the chillies in the batter and deep fry for 2 minutes. Remove and place on a rack over a plate and leave to drain.

Leave to cool for about 5 minutes. (The chillies can be refrigerated for up to 24 hours at this stage.)

Dip the chillies in the besan and rice flour batter again and fry until golden brown. Serve immediately.

7

LAMB DISHES

Menu

LAMB CURRY – Mild, Madras, or vindaloo.

BHUNA GHOST – Lamb cooked in spices and flavoured with green herbs.

LAMB PASANDA – Marinated lamb pieces in a mild creamy sauce with nuts.

LAMB DOPIAZA – Lamb cooked with onions and spices.

SHAHI KORMA – Lamb cooked in cream, spices, and nuts, mildly spiced.

ROGAN JOSH – Lamb cooked with yogurt, spices, and nuts.

LAMB DHANSAK – Lamb with lentils.

SAG MEAT – Lamb cooked with spinach and spices.

KEEMA PEAS – Minced lamb cooked with spices and peas.

NARGIS KEBAB CURRY – Hard-boiled eggs, encased in moist spicy minced lamb, pan fried and served with a creamy sauce.

LAMB SHASLIK – Marinated pieces of tender meat and fresh vegetables, lightly spiced, skewered and grilled to perfection.

Preparation of Lamb

Lamb is generally the only red meat used by Indian restaurants. The use of beef or pork is largely avoided, as certain ethnic groups will not eat one or the other.

For our lamb curries we use leg of spring lamb, either fresh or frozen, according to season. The quality of your lamb dishes will depend heavily on the quality and preparation of the meat. It is essential to buy tender spring lamb and remove – or have removed by your butcher – all bone, fat and gristle. Cut the remaining lean meat into one inch (2.5cm) cubes (except for lamb pasanda) and you are ready to proceed.

NB. All the recipes in this book are for boned lamb. If you prefer your meat unboned you may use it in this way, but remember to double the quantity.

Preparation and cooking time: 45 minutes.
For 6–8 people you will need:

2 lb (900g) lamb, prepared as above
8 tbsp vegetable oil
1 tsp turmeric
4 tbsp reserved curry sauce, prepared to the end of stage 2 (page 20)

Wash and drain the meat. Place the oil, turmeric and curry sauce in a large saucepan and mix well. Cook on a medium heat, stirring continuously until the sauce begins to darken in colour (4–5 minutes). Add the meat and stir until all the pieces are well coated. Turn down the heat and cook, covered, for 30–40 minutes or until the meat is tender, stirring every few minutes to ensure even cooking.

Remove the lamb pieces, leaving behind the sediment, and place in a clean container. The lamb may now be used immediately for any of the curries in this chapter, as well as lamb biryani (but not for balti meat).

Or it can be cooled and refrigerated for up to 4 days. If refrigerating, skim the oil from the sediment and pour onto the meat to keep it moist.

Freezing: Freeze for up to 2 months.

LAMB CURRY

This is a basic lamb curry which is simple to make. Vary the chilli according to taste for a mild to medium to very hot curry, or use a combination of chilli powder and green chillies for more flavour.

Serves 3–4.
Preparation and cooking time: 15 minutes.

5 tbsp vegetable oil
3 UK cups (2 US cups/15 fl oz/425ml) curry sauce (page 20)
1 tsp salt
½ tsp chilli powder
1 lb (450g) cooked lamb (page 65)
1 level tsp garam masala
½ level tsp ground cumin
Pinch of dried, ground fenugreek leaves (optional)
1 tbsp finely chopped green coriander

Heat the oil in a large, deep frying pan, add the curry sauce and bring to the boil.

Continue to cook on a high heat and add the salt, chilli powder and the cooked lamb. Mix well and cook for about 5 minutes.

Turn down the heat to a simmer and stir in the garam masala, ground cumin, and dried fenugreek. Simmer for a further 6–7 minutes.

Skim off any excess oil. Sprinkle on the coriander just before serving.

BHUNA GHOST

This is a deliciously spicy lamb dish and a firm favourite. Adjust the amount of chilli used according to taste.

Serves 3–4.
Preparation and cooking time: 15–20 minutes.

2 oz (50g) mushrooms
½ green capsicum
6 tbsp vegetable oil
3 UK cups (2 US cups/15 fl oz/425ml) curry sauce (page 20)
1 lb (450g) cooked lamb (page 65)
1 tsp salt
½ tsp chilli powder
1 green chilli, finely chopped
¼ tsp red food colouring
1½ tsp garam masala
1 tsp ground cumin
½ level tsp dried, ground fenugreek leaves
1 tbsp finely chopped green coriander

Wash the mushrooms and capsicum and slice thinly.

Heat the oil in a large, deep frying pan and fry for 4–5 minutes on a medium heat.

Add the curry sauce, lamb, salt, chilli powder and chilli, and food colouring. Turn up the heat and bring to the boil. Continue cooking for 5 minutes, stirring frequently.

Now turn down the heat slightly and stir in the garam masala, ground cumin and fenugreek and cook for a further 5 minutes, stirring now and again.

Spoon off any excess oil and sprinkle on the green coriander before serving.

LAMB PASANDA

The lamb for this dish will need to be prepared in advance as it requires marinating.

Serves 3–4.
Marinating time: 2 hours.
Preparation and cooking time: 35–40 minutes.

1 lb (450g) lean lamb
1 UK cup (⅔ US cup/5 fl oz/150ml) plain yogurt
1½ tsp salt
4 tbsp vegetable oil
3 UK cups (2 US cups/15 fl oz/425ml) curry sauce (page 20)
1 tsp paprika
½ tsp garam masala
1 tsp ground cumin
1 tbsp roughly chopped cashew nuts (optional)
4 tbsp double cream
1 tbsp finely chopped green coriander

Wash the meat and cut into slices about ¼ inch (0.5cm) thick and 3 inches (7.5cm) by 2 inches (5cm). Boil in salted water for 15 minutes until the meat is tender.

Mix the yogurt and ½ teaspoonful salt in a bowl and add the meat slices whilst still hot. Stir, coating the meat well, and marinate for at least 2 hours or up to 24 hours.

Heat the oil in a large, deep frying pan. Pour in the sauce and bring it to the boil. Stir in 1 teaspoonful salt and the paprika and cook on a high heat for 5 minutes, stirring frequently.

Now turn down the heat and stir in the garam masala, cumin and nuts. Also add the meat, shaking off as much of the yogurt as you can. Stir and simmer for 5 minutes or so.

Spoon off any oil, and stir in the cream and half the coriander. Simmer for a minute.

Sprinkle the remaining coriander on top just before serving.

LAMB DOPIAZA

This is a mildly spiced lamb dish cooked with onions.

Serves 3–4.
Preparation and cooking time: 15 minutes.

6 tbsp vegetable oil
2 small onions, peeled and cut into rings
3 UK cups (2 US cups/15 fl oz/425ml) curry sauce (page 20)
1 tsp salt
1 level tsp chilli powder
1 lb (425g) cooked lamb (page 65)
1 level tsp garam masala
1 level tsp ground cumin
½ level tsp ground coriander
½ level tsp dried, ground fenugreek leaves
1 tbsp finely chopped green coriander

Heat the oil in a large, deep frying pan. Add the sliced onions and fry until transparent. Pour in the curry sauce, mix well and bring to a simmer.

Stir in the salt, chilli powder, and lamb. Cook on a medium heat for 10 minutes, or until the sauce is quite thick, stirring now and again.

Now stir in the garam masala, cumin, ground coriander, and fenugreek. Continue to cook for 3–4 minutes.

Skim off excess oil and sprinkle with the green coriander before serving.

SHAHI KORMA

This is a delicious creamy lamb dish.

Serves 3–4.
Preparation and cooking time: 15 minutes.

4 tbsp vegetable oil
3 UK cups (2 US cups/15 fl oz/425ml) curry sauce (page 20)
1 lb (450g) cooked lamb (page 65)
2 tbsp cashew nuts, roughly chopped
1½ tsp salt
¼ tsp yellow food colouring
½ tsp garam masala
1 tsp ground cumin
1 UK cup (⅔ US cup/5 fl oz/150ml) single cream
2 tsp finely chopped green coriander

Heat the oil in a large, deep frying pan and add to it the curry sauce.
Bring to the boil on a high heat.

Without turning down the heat, add the lamb, cashew nuts, salt, and
food colouring. Stir, and cook for 5 minutes or so, stirring frequently.

Turn down the heat slightly and cook for a further 5 minutes. Stir
in the garam masala and ground cumin.

Now stir in the cream and heat gently for 3–4 minutes, stirring all
the time.

Serve sprinkled with the green coriander.

ROGAN JOSH

This is probably the most popular of all the lamb dishes.

Serves 3–4.
Preparation and cooking time: 15 minutes.

6 tbsp vegetable oil
3 UK cups (2 US cups/15 fl oz/425ml) curry sauce (page 20)
1 lb (450g) cooked lamb (page 65)
2 tsp paprika
1 tsp chilli powder
1 tsp salt
1 tbsp cashew nuts (optional)
1 tsp garam masala
1 tsp ground cumin
2 tbsp plain yogurt, beaten smooth
2 tsp finely chopped green coriander

Heat the oil in a large, deep frying pan, add to it the curry sauce and bring to the boil.

Without reducing the heat, add the meat, paprika, chilli powder, salt and cashew nuts (if used). Stir well and cook for 5 minutes, stirring frequently.

Now turn down the heat and, whilst the meat is simmering, stir in the garam masala and ground cumin. Slowly add the yogurt, mixing all the time and cooking for a further 3 or 4 minutes. There should now be a dark thick sauce, reddish brown in colour.

Allow to settle and spoon off any excess oil. Serve sprinkled with the green coriander.

LAMB DHANSAK

This is a lamb curry combined with lentil dal. A hot, sour dish, it sometimes has pineapple chunks added to it. Stir these in just before serving if you wish to try it this way.

Serves 3–4.
Preparation and cooking time: 20–25 minutes.

6 tbsp vegetable oil
2 UK cups (1¼ US cups/10 fl oz/275ml) curry sauce (page 20)
2 UK cups (1¼ US cups) lentil dal (page 94)
1 lb (450g) cooked lamb (page 65)
½ tsp salt
½ tsp chilli powder
1 green chilli, finely chopped
1½ tsp garam masala
1 tsp ground cumin
2 tbsp lemon juice
1 tbsp finely chopped green coriander

Heat the oil in a large, deep frying pan. Add the curry sauce and lentil dal and bring to the boil.

Without turning down the heat, add the lamb, salt, chilli powder and green chilli.

Stir well and continue to cook on a high heat for about 5 minutes, or until the sauce thickens, stirring regularly.

Now turn down the heat to a simmer for a further 5 minutes, stirring now and again.

Skim off any excess oil and stir in the garam masala, ground cumin and lemon juice.

Serve sprinkled with the green coriander.

SAG MEAT

This dish is an interesting combination of lamb and spinach.

Serves 4.
Preparation and cooking time: 20–25 minutes.

6 tbsp vegetable oil
3 UK cups (2 US cups/15 fl oz/425ml) curry sauce (page 20)
16 oz (450g) can puréed spinach
1 tsp salt
1 tsp chilli powder
1 green chilli, finely chopped (optional)
1 lb (450g) cooked lamb (page 65)
1½ tsp garam masala
2 tsp finely chopped green coriander

Heat the oil in a large, deep frying pan. Add the curry sauce and spinach, stir and bring to the boil.

Stir in the salt, chilli powder, and green chilli (if used) and continue to cook until the mixture thickens, stirring frequently. This will take about 10–15 minutes.

Now add the lamb and the garam masala and simmer on a low heat for a further 5 minutes, stirring now and again.

Take off the heat before stirring in the coriander.

KEEMA PEAS

This is a dish consisting of lean minced lamb and garden peas.

Serves 4.
Preparation and cooking time: 40–45 minutes.

4 tbsp vegetable oil
1 lb (450g) minced lamb
2 UK cups (1¼ US cups/10 fl oz/275ml) curry sauce (page 20)
½ lb (225g) frozen peas
1 tsp salt
1 tsp ground cumin
½ tsp chilli powder
½ green chilli, finely chopped
1 tsp garam masala
2 tsp finely chopped green coriander

Heat the oil in a large, deep frying pan on a medium heat, add the minced lamb and cook, stirring, until browned. Turn down the heat and cook covered for 10 minutes.

Now add the curry sauce, peas, salt, ground cumin, chilli powder and green chilli. Stir and bring the sauce to a simmer. Continue to simmer uncovered for about 30 minutes.

Stir in the garam masala and cook for a minute. Take off the heat before stirring in the green coriander.

NARGIS KEBAB CURRY

Serves 4.
Preparation and cooking time: 20–25 minutes.

2 tbsp oil
1 x 2 inch (5cm) stick cinnamon
6 cloves
6 green cardamom pods, crushed
½ x 400g can tomatoes
3 UK cups (2 US cups/15 fl oz/425ml) curry sauce (page 20)
1 tsp chilli powder
½ tsp salt
4 tbsp plain yogurt
½ tsp garam masala
4 nargis kebabs (page 28)
2 tbsp chopped coriander

Heat the oil in a deep frying pan and add the cinnamon, cloves, and cardamoms and fry for 30 seconds.

Add the tomatoes to the pan, and gently crush them down, and cook, stirring, for about 5 minutes until the tomatoes are thick and pulpy.

Add the curry sauce, chilli powder and salt, and bring to the boil. Turn down the heat a little and continue to cook, stirring until reduced and thick.

Stir in the yogurt, a spoonful at a time. Make sure each spoonful is absorbed and it is smooth before adding the next spoonful. Stir in the garam masala.

Add the kebabs to the sauce, gently turn them in the sauce, bring to a simmer and heat through, covered, for a few minutes.

Sprinkle on the coriander and serve.

LAMB SHASLIK

Marinated pieces of tender meat, spiced, skewered and grilled to perfection, are combined with grilled fresh vegetables to make this irresistible food. You can use chicken fillet instead of lamb if you prefer.

Chef's tip: Prepare and marinate the meat the night before for extra flavour and a quick meal the next day.

Serves 3–4.
Marinating time: 2 hours.
Preparation and cooking time: 20–25 minutes.

1 lb (500g) of lamb leg meat, cut into 1 inch (2.5cm) cubes
1 bay leaf
2 tbsp vegetable oil
1 tbsp lemon juice
2 large cloves of garlic, finely chopped
1 tsp ground cumin
½ tsp ground chilli
½ tsp freshly ground black pepper
1 tbsp coriander stalks, chopped finely
2 tomatoes, quartered
1 onion, cut into wedges
1 small green capsicum, cut into 1 inch (2.5cm) squares
1 red capsicum, cut into 1 inch (2.5cm) squares
1 tsp salt

Place the lamb and the bay leaf in a non-metallic bowl.

Combine the oil, lemon juice, garlic, cumin, chilli, pepper and coriander in a screw-top jar or cup and shake or mix with a fork until combined.

Pour over the meat and mix thoroughly until the meat is well coated. Cover and refrigerate for 2 hours.

Thirty minutes or so before you are ready to cook, remove the marinated meat from the fridge and mix in the vegetables. If you are using wooden skewers, place in water to soak.

Preheat the grill to very hot. Sprinkle the salt over the meat and vegetables, and mix again. Thread the meat and vegetables onto the skewers, alternating a piece of meat with a piece of vegetable, and brush with the remaining marinade.

Grill as close as possible to the griller, for about 8–10 minutes, turning once. Serve with yogurt mint sauce (page 17), or plain yogurt and rice.

8

BALTI DISHES

Menu

BALTI CHICKEN

BALTI MEAT

BALTI CHICKEN PASANDA

I can think of few things in Indian cookery more mouth-watering than the delicious sound of a sizzling tandoori starter or balti curry. Although the concept of the balti dish is simple, its allure is remarkable. That unmistakable sizzle and aroma as you are served your meal, still simmering from the kitchen in its individual balti, make these dishes exceptionally popular. And so they should be. With a generous combination of succulent pieces of meat or chicken, onions, and capsicums, all smothered in a dark, thick, and spicy sauce, these dishes are amongst the best from the restaurant menu.

The balti is another name for the Indian karahi, a utensil similar to the Chinese wok. The sizzle is produced by putting the hot curry into a preheated balti. The oily sauce comes into contact with the hot surface and causes the sizzling.

You will need to buy the baltis or karahis if you wish to serve these dishes in the traditional way. It is not essential, but you will require them if you want authenticity. Baltis can be found in many Asian stores and are relatively inexpensive to buy. In their absence any metal utensil such as a small frying pan or saucepan would do.

BALTI CHICKEN

Serves 2–3.
Preparation and cooking time: 20–25 minutes.

3 chicken fillets
4 tbsp vegetable oil, plus more for deep frying
3 UK cups (2 US cups/15 fl oz/425ml) curry sauce (page 20)
Red food colouring (optional)
1 tsp salt
½ tsp chilli powder
1 medium-sized onion
1 green capsicum
1½ tsp garam masala
1 tsp ground cumin
1 tbsp finely chopped green coriander

Cut each chicken fillet into 4 strips, wash and drain.

Heat the oil in a large, deep frying pan and put the chicken pieces into it. Sauté for 4–5 minutes on a medium heat.

Pour the curry sauce into the pan with the chicken and bring to the boil on a high heat. Turn down the heat to medium.

Now add the food colouring, salt, and chilli powder. Stir and leave to simmer for 12–15 minutes, stirring now and again.

Meanwhile, peel and wash the onion. Slice into two halves and then quarter each half. Set aside.

Wash the capsicum, slice lengthways into two and deseed. Now cut each half into 2 strips and each strip into 3 pieces across.

Heat the oil for deep frying. When hot add the onion and capsicum. Fry for 2–3 minutes until the onion is just beginning to brown. Remove with a slotted spoon and drain on kitchen paper.

When the chicken has been simmering for 12 minutes or so, add the fried onion and capsicum to it.

Continue cooking on a medium heat until the sauce becomes quite thick, about 5 minutes or so.

Stir in the garam masala and ground cumin and turn the heat to very low. The oil will start to rise to the surface where it can be skimmed off if desired.

While the chicken is still on a low heat, heat the baltis. This can be done on top of the hob for about 30 seconds.

When you have done this, immediately spoon in the curry. It will start sizzling and simmering in the balti.

Quickly sprinkle on the coriander and serve.

NB. If you do not get the sizzling when you put the curry in the baltis, it is probably because you have not heated them sufficiently. They need to be quite hot and not just warm. Leave the curry simmering while you heat the baltis. It is the combination of the piping hot curry and very hot balti that causes the sizzling.

BALTI MEAT

Follow the recipe for Balti Chicken, replacing the chicken with 1 lb (450g) cooked lamb for 2–3 people. You will not need to sauté the cooked meat, so omit that stage of the method and simply put the sauce and meat into the hot oil and proceed from there.

It will be necessary for you to read page 65 on how to prepare the lamb, but remember that there is a larger quantity of meat in balti meat than in other curries and allow approximately 1 lb (450g) of lean meat for two or three people, instead of for three or four as in other recipes. Also when cutting the meat into cubes make them a little larger than the one inch (2.5cm) recommended. This is ideal but not essential, so if you have some cooked lamb in the freezer that you have kept for curries, you may use it in balti meat.

BALTI CHICKEN PASANDA

This balti dish requires some time for marinating but is well worth the wait. It has a delicious thick sauce and is wonderful eaten with fruity pilau (page 109) and plain nan bread.

Chef's tip: Marinate the chicken the night before for a quick and tasty meal the next evening.

Serves 4–6.
Marinating time: 3–4 hours (or overnight).
Preparation and cooking time: 35–40 minutes.

1 lb (450g) chicken fillets
4 tbsp thick plain yogurt
½ tsp turmeric
½ tbsp black cumin seeds
4 cardamom pods, crushed
6 whole black peppercorns
1 tbsp garam masala
1 tbsp ground almonds
2 cloves of garlic, finely chopped
1 tsp chilli powder
½ tsp salt
1 tsp paprika
2 tbsp vegetable oil or ghee
3 UK cups (2 US cups/15 fl oz/425 ml) curry sauce (page 20)
2 fresh green chillies, finely chopped
4 tbsp single cream
1 tbsp chopped fresh coriander

Wash the chicken and wipe dry with paper towels. Slice each fillet into 4–5 slices of even size.

In a medium non-metallic bowl, mix the yogurt, turmeric, cumin seeds, cardamoms, peppercorns, *2 teaspoons* of the garam masala, ground almonds, garlic, chilli powder, salt and paprika. Add the chicken pieces and leave to marinate in the fridge, for 3–4 hours or overnight.

Heat the oil in a large, deep frying pan, stir in the curry sauce and bring to the boil. Turn down the heat a little and continue cooking and stirring until the sauce has thickened – about 5 minutes.

Add the chicken mixture and stir to coat with the sauce. Cook over a medium heat for about 15 minutes, stirring frequently, until the sauce thickens again and is beginning to release the oil and the chicken is cooked through. Take care that it doesn't catch on the bottom of the pan and add a little water if the sauce is thickening too quickly.

Add the green chillies and the cream. Bring back to a simmer and simmer gently for a couple of minutes. Stir in the remaining garam masala and the coriander and serve garnished with more fresh coriander, if desired.

9

FISH DISHES

Menu

PRAWN CURRY

BHUNA PRAWN

PRAWN AND MUSHROOM

TANDOORI KING PRAWN MASALA

TANDOORI FISH MASALA

PRAWN PATIA

Indian restaurants are often not very adventurous when it comes to fish, relying mainly on prawns for the fish dishes on the menu. I have included these popular prawn dishes in this chapter and also one using cod. You may, however, like to experiment with other varieties like haddock, plaice, mackerel or any firm white fleshed fish. Simply remember to cook the fish first and either stir it into the sauce of your choice or pour the sauce over the fish just before serving.

A word about prawns. I have said in an earlier chapter that we buy king prawns that are uncooked and frozen in their shells. Fresh, uncooked prawns appear not to be readily available so this is the next best choice. Using freshly cooked rather than pre-cooked prawns is by far the best way and the difference is quite noticeable.

PRAWN CURRY

Use king prawns or the smaller variety as you prefer. If using uncooked king prawns, cook them in boiling salted water for 5 minutes and cut each prawn in half before using.

Remember, you can produce a prawn Madras or vindaloo simply by increasing the amount of chilli powder.

Serves 3–4.
Preparation and cooking time: 10–15 minutes.

4 tbsp vegetable oil
3 UK cups (2 US cups/15 fl oz/425ml) curry sauce (page 20)
½ tsp salt
Pinch of chilli powder or to taste
½ tsp ground coriander
12 oz (350g) peeled prawns, defrosted as necessary
½ tsp garam masala
1 tbsp finely chopped green coriander

Heat the oil in a large, deep frying pan and pour in the curry sauce. Bring to the boil and cook on a medium-high heat for about 5 minutes until you have a thick sauce.

Stir in all the remaining ingredients, except for the green coriander, and simmer, stirring frequently, for 4 or 5 minutes.

Sprinkle the green coriander over just before serving.

BHUNA PRAWN

This is a spicy prawn dish with a good, thick sauce. Remember to cook uncooked prawns for 5 minutes in boiling salted water and to slice king prawns into two before using.

Serves 3–4.
Preparation and cooking time: 15–20 minutes.

2 oz (50g) button mushrooms
½ green capsicum
6 tbsp vegetable oil
3 UK cups (2 US cups/15 fl oz/425ml) curry sauce (page 20)
1 tsp salt
½ tsp chilli powder
1 tsp cumin
1½ tsp garam masala
12 oz (350g) peeled prawns, defrosted as necessary
½ level tsp dried, ground fenugreek leaves
1 tbsp finely chopped green coriander

Rinse the mushrooms and capsicum and slice thinly. Heat the oil in a large, deep frying pan and fry them for 4–5 minutes on a medium heat.

Now add the curry sauce, salt, chilli powder, and cumin. Turn up the heat and bring to the boil.

Cook the sauce on a high heat, stirring frequently, until it is really thick.

Stir in the garam masala, prawns, and dried fenugreek and simmer for 3 minutes.

Drain off excess oil and sprinkle with the green coriander before serving.

PRAWN AND MUSHROOM

As with the other prawn dishes in this chapter, use either king prawns or small prawns. Cook uncooked king prawns in boiling salted water for 5 minutes and cut into two pieces before using.

Serves 4.
Preparation and cooking time: 15–20 minutes.

4 oz (110g) button mushrooms
6 tbsp vegetable oil
3 UK cups (2 US cups/15 fl oz/425ml) curry sauce (page 20)
1 tsp salt
½ tsp chilli powder
½ tsp ground coriander
12 oz (350g) peeled prawns, defrosted as necessary
1 tsp garam masala
1 tbsp finely chopped green coriander

Rinse and halve, quarter, or thickly slice the mushrooms according to size.

Heat the oil in a large, deep frying pan and fry the mushrooms on a medium heat for 4 minutes.

Add the curry sauce, salt, chilli powder, and ground coriander.

Bring the sauce to the boil on a high heat and cook for around 5 minutes until thickened.

Now add the prawns and garam masala and simmer for 3 minutes.

Drain off excess oil and serve sprinkled with the green coriander.

TANDOORI KING PRAWN MASALA

This is a delicious, creamy dish using king prawns that have been cooked tandoori style.

Serves 3–4.
Preparation and cooking time: 15 minutes.

4 tbsp vegetable oil
3 UK cups (2 US cups/15 fl oz/425ml) curry sauce (page 20)
1 tsp salt
1 tsp paprika
½ tsp chilli powder
Pinch of red food colouring
1 level tsp garam masala
½ tsp ground cumin
16 king prawns, freshly cooked tandoori style (page 36)
6 tbsp single cream
1 tbsp finely chopped green coriander

Heat the oil in a large, deep frying pan, add the curry sauce and bring to the boil.

Add the salt, paprika, chilli powder and food colouring and cook the sauce, stirring, on a medium-high heat for about 5 minutes until it is quite thick.

Reduce the heat and stir in the garam masala and cumin powder. Simmer for 3 minutes.

Spoon off any excess oil. Cut each prawn in half and add them to the sauce. Stir in the cream and heat through for 2 minutes. Serve sprinkled with the green coriander.

TANDOORI FISH MASALA

This dish is made in the same way as the tandoori king prawn masala. Substitute the tandoori king prawns with tandoori fish (page 35), allowing around 12 oz (350g) for 3–4 people.

PRAWN PATIA

A delectable combination of hot, sweet and sour, Patia is a dish brought to India by the Parsees a thousand years ago. Traditionally made with fish or prawns, although chicken and lamb versions are now popular. Substitute cubed firm white fish for the prawns if you prefer.

Serves 4.
Preparation and cooking time: 20 minutes.

1 lb (450g) peeled uncooked prawns, defrosted if using frozen
3 tbsp vegetable oil
1 tsp chilli powder
1 tsp ground coriander
½ tsp ground cumin
½ tsp turmeric
3 UK cups (2 US cups/15 fl oz/425ml) curry sauce (page 20)
1 heaped tsp jaggery (or dark brown sugar)
1 heaped tsp tamarind purée (or 1–2 tbsp lemon juice)
1 tsp salt

Wash the prawns and wipe dry with paper towels. In a non-metallic bowl, mix 1 tablespoonful of the oil with the chilli powder, ground coriander, cumin and turmeric. Add the prawns, and mix well until coated with the spices. Set aside.

Heat the remaining oil in a deep frying pan and add the curry sauce, bring to the boil and simmer for about 5 minutes until reduced and thick. It should be releasing the oil.

Dissolve the jaggery, or sugar, and tamarind, or lemon juice, in a little hot water and add to the sauce. Cook for a minute more. Taste, adding a little more tamarind/lemon juice, sugar, chilli and salt so that the hot, sweet, sour taste is to your liking.

Heat another frying pan until hot, and add the prawns. Stir fry for a minute or so and add the prawns to the sauce. Bring back to a simmer and serve immediately.

10

VEGETABLE DISHES

Menu

BENGAN BHAJI – Aubergine cooked in spices.

ALOO GOBI – Potatoes and cauliflower in spices.

CHANA ALOO – Chickpeas cooked with potatoes.

MUSHROOMS AND PEAS – Mushrooms and peas in a spicy sauce.

BHINDI BHAJI – Okra cooked with onion and spices.

TARKA DAL – Lentils with herbs and spices.

STUFFED CHILLI PEPPER (VEGETARIAN) – Mild, peppery banana chillies, stuffed with spicy potatoes, dipped in batter and deep fried until crisp and golden.

MATTAR PANIR – Cottage cheese with peas in a spicy sauce.

SAG PANIR – Spinach with cottage cheese cubes.

MIXED VEGETABLES – Fresh garden vegetables with herbs and spices.

BENGAN BHAJI

Aubergines are best cooked in plenty of hot oil and this dish demands that you do not skimp on the oil during cooking although you may strain it off afterwards.

Buy plump aubergines with an even shiny purple colour.

Serves 4–6.
Preparation and cooking time: 30–35 minutes.

1 lb (450g) aubergines
1 small green capsicum
1 onion
1 tsp salt
½ tsp chilli powder
1 tsp garam masala
1 UK cup (⅔ US cup/5 fl oz/150ml) vegetable oil

Wash and cut the aubergines lengthwise into quarters, and then cut into about 1 inch (2.5cm) thick wedges.

Cut the capsicum in a similar way, and peel and chop the onion coarsely, separating the slices.

Place all the vegetables into a bowl and sprinkle on the salt and the spices and mix well.

Heat the oil in a karahi or deep pan. When hot put in the vegetables and cook, stirring frequently, on a medium heat for 10 minutes.

Turn down the heat slightly and cook for a further 10–15 minutes until the aubergine wedges are soft but still hold their shape.

Allow the oil to settle for a few minutes and drain off if desired.

Serve hot.

ALOO GOBI

This is a popular dish of cauliflower and potatoes.

Serves 4.
Preparation and cooking time: 40–45 minutes.

8 oz (225g) potatoes
1 small cauliflower
4 tbsp vegetable oil
½ tsp ground cumin
1 UK cup (⅔ US cup/5 fl oz/150ml) curry sauce (page 20)
1 level tsp salt
½ tsp ground coriander
½ tsp turmeric
1 green chilli, finely chopped
2 tsp finely chopped green coriander

Boil or microwave the potatoes in their jackets and leave until cool enough to handle.

Break up the cauliflower into florets. Rinse and drain.

Heat the oil in a heavy-based pan. When hot add the ground cumin. Almost immediately add the cauliflower.

Cook, stirring on a medium heat, for 2–3 minutes.

Now add the curry sauce, salt, ground coriander, turmeric, and chilli. Mix well and cook partly covered on a low heat for about 20 minutes or until the cauliflower is just tender. Stir frequently during this time.

Whilst the cauliflower is cooking, peel the potatoes and cut into 1 inch (2.5cm) dice.

Add the potatoes to the cooked cauliflower and stir gently to prevent them breaking. Heat though for 3 or 4 minutes.

Stir in the green coriander and serve.

CHANA ALOO

Chana or chickpeas are available ready cooked in cans from most supermarkets. Many restaurants buy them this way as they are good and convenient. If you buy them uncooked, they will need to be soaked for 24 hours and then simmered for about an hour to an hour and a half until tender.

Serves 3–4.
Preparation and cooking time: 20–25 minutes.

8 oz (225g) potatoes
15 oz (425g) can chickpeas in brine
5 tbsp vegetable oil
2 UK cups (1¼ US cups/10 fl oz/275ml) curry sauce (page 20)
2 tsp tomato purée
1 tsp salt
1 tsp ground cumin
1 tsp ground coriander
1 tsp garam masala
1 tsp chilli powder
½ tsp amchoor (or 2 tbsp lemon juice) *← too much? half*
½ level tsp dried, ground fenugreek leaves
2 tsp finely chopped green coriander

Boil or microwave the potatoes in their skins. Cool slightly, peel, and cut into 1 inch (2.5cm) dice.

Drain and rinse the chickpeas in a colander.

Heat the oil in a heavy pan, add the curry sauce, and boil for about 5 minutes until thickened.

Stir in all the remaining ingredients except the potatoes and green coriander, and simmer gently for 5 minutes, stirring frequently.

Add the potatoes, heat through for 4 or 5 minutes, and stir in the green coriander.

MUSHROOMS AND PEAS

This delicious dish is not often found in restaurants, but one that is definitely worth trying. Halve, quarter, or thickly slice the mushrooms according to their size.

Serves 3–4.
Preparation and cooking time: 30 minutes.

12 oz (350g) button mushrooms
8 oz (225g) frozen peas
4 tbsp vegetable oil
1½ UK cups (1 US cup/8 fl oz/200ml) curry sauce (page 20)
1 level tsp salt
½ tsp turmeric
½ tsp ground cumin
½ tsp chilli powder
½ level tsp dried, ground fenugreek leaves
½ tsp garam masala
2 tsp finely chopped green coriander

Rinse and thickly slice the mushrooms. Rinse the frozen peas well in hot water and drain.

Heat the oil in a deep frying pan. When hot, add the mushrooms and cook on a gentle heat for 3–4 minutes.

Add the peas and cook for 5 minutes.

Now add the curry sauce and bring to a simmer. Stir in the salt, turmeric, ground cumin, and chilli powder.

Simmer, stirring occasionally, for about 15 minutes.

Add the dried fenugreek and the garam masala and simmer for a further 5 minutes.

Allow the oil to settle and skim off the excess. Stir in the green coriander and serve.

BHINDI BHAJI

This is probably the most popular of the vegetable dishes served by Indian restaurants.

Buy fresh okra and look for young tender pods.

Serves 4.
Preparation and cooking time: 20–25 minutes.

12 oz (350g) okra
Oil for deep frying
3 tbsp vegetable oil
1 UK cup (⅔ US cup/5 fl oz/150ml) curry sauce (page 20)
1 level tsp salt
½–1 tsp chilli powder
1 tsp ground cumin
1 tsp ground coriander
½ tsp garam masala
3 tsp lemon juice

Wash the okra and pat dry. Top and tail the pods and cut into ¾ inch (2cm) lengths.

Heat the oil for deep frying and fry the okra for 7–8 minutes. Drain.

Heat the 3 tablespoonfuls of oil in a deep frying pan and pour in the curry sauce. Bring it to the boil and cook on a high heat until it becomes quite thick.

Turn down the heat and stir in the salt and spices. Add the okra to the pan and mix well.

Cook uncovered for about 3 minutes and sprinkle on the lemon juice.

Serve hot.

TARKA DAL

This nutritious dal is made with red split lentils which turn a pale yellow when cooked.

Serves 4–6 as a side dish ?!? It so the lot for lunch
Preparation and cooking time: 1 hour.

4 heaped tbsp red split lentils
3 UK cups (2 US cups/15 fl oz/425ml) water
1 level tsp salt
1 small onion, chopped
3 cloves of garlic, finely chopped
4 tbsp melted vegetable ghee
Pinch of turmeric
½ tsp garam masala
1 small tomato
2 tsp finely chopped green coriander

Pick over the lentils for any stones and wash them in several changes of water. Put into a saucepan with the cups of water, add the salt, and bring to the boil.

Turn down the heat and simmer uncovered, skimming off the froth that collects at the top for the first 20 minutes or so during cooking. After this stage, the pan should be partly covered.

Cook, stirring occasionally, for a total time of 1 hour, at the end of which time you should have a pale yellow, souplike consistency.

While the dal is cooking, fry the onion and garlic in the ghee until the onion is pale brown.

Add the turmeric and garam masala to the onion and cook for 2 or 3 seconds.

Stir the onion mixture into the cooked lentils. Serve hot, sprinkled with chopped tomato and green coriander.

STUFFED CHILLI PEPPER (VEGETARIAN)

The large yellowish-green chilli peppers, sometimes known as banana chillies, used for this dish have a mild peppery taste and are less fleshy than capsicum. Delicious served as a starter or side dish, this is a great way to use up left-over mashed potato!

Chef's tip: the chillies can be kept for up to 24 hours after the first frying. The batter will become a little thinner on standing – thicken it by mixing in a dessertspoon or so of besan flour.

Serves 4.
Preparation and cooking time: 15–20 minutes.

8 banana chillies
1 UK cup (⅔ US cup) cooked mashed potato
Salt to taste
½–1 tsp red chilli powder
½ tsp turmeric
½ tsp garam masala
1 tsp cumin powder
1 tsp amchoor (or juice of ½ lemon)
2 tbsp chopped coriander leaves
1½ UK cups (1 US cup) besan flour
2 tbsp rice flour
¼ tsp baking soda
Oil for deep frying

Wash the chillies and wipe dry. Slit each chilli along its length, leaving about ½ an inch (1cm) each end intact. Carefully open up the chilli and, using a teaspoon, scrape out the seeds and ribs.

Mix the mashed potato with salt, the chilli powder, turmeric, garam masala, cumin powder, amchoor or lemon juice, and coriander leaves.

Using small portions at a time, stuff the chillies with this mixture, taking care not to rip the flesh. Do not overfill.

Mix the besan flour, rice flour, half a teaspoonful of salt and the baking soda in a medium-sized bowl. Add enough cold water to make a coating batter, approximately the consistency of single cream.

Heat some oil in a karahi or deep pan until moderately hot (when the surface of the oil starts to shimmer). Dip the chillies in the batter and deep fry for 2 minutes. Remove and place on a rack over a plate and leave to drain.

Leave to cool for about 5 minutes.

Dip the chillies in the besan and rice flour batter again and fry until golden brown. Serve hot with yogurt mint sauce (page 17).

MATTAR PANIR

This is a dish that is popular with vegetarians as it contains plenty of protein in the form of curd cheese cubes.

Serves 2–3.
Preparation and cooking time: 40–45 minutes

2 UK pints (2½ US pints/1.15 litres) whole milk
4 tbsp lemon juice
Oil for deep frying
6 oz (175g) frozen peas
4 tbsp vegetable oil
2 UK cups (1¼ US cups/10 fl oz/275ml) curry sauce (page 20)
1 level tsp salt
½ tsp turmeric
½ tsp ground coriander
½ tsp chilli powder
½ tsp garam masala
1 tbsp single cream (optional)
2 tsp finely chopped green coriander

Bring the milk to the boil in a saucepan. Immediately add the lemon juice and stir until the milk appears to curdle. The solids should be visibly separated from the whey.

Strain though muslin or a clean tea towel. Place the curds, still in muslin, in a tray. Put something flat on it, such as a chopping board, and weigh it down with something heavy. A large saucepan full of water is ideal. Leave for about 15 minutes. This squeezes all the liquid out of the curds.

When this is done, cut the fat slab of curds into approximately ½ inch (1cm) cubes, and deep fry in hot oil until golden on the outside. Drain.

Rinse the frozen peas in hot water and drain. Heat the oil in a deep frying pan and fry the peas in it for about 3 minutes.

Add the curry sauce and bring to a simmer. Stir in the salt, turmeric, ground coriander, and chilli powder and simmer for 10 minutes.

Now add the cheese cubes and the garam masala. Simmer for a further 10 minutes.

Stir in the cream if used, and the green coriander.

SAG PANIR

Here curd cheese cubes are combined with spicy spinach.

Serves 3–4.
Preparation and cooking time: 40–45 minutes.

2 UK pints (2½ US pints/1.15 litres) whole milk
4 tbsp lemon juice
Oil for deep frying
4 tbsp vegetable oil
1 UK cup (⅔ US cup/5 fl oz/150ml) curry sauce (page 20)
16 oz (450g) can puréed spinach
½ tsp salt
1 tsp ground cumin
½ tsp chilli powder
1 tsp garam masala

Make the milk into curd cheese cubes as explained opposite for mattar panir.

Heat the 4 tablespoonfuls of oil in a deep frying pan.

When hot add the curry sauce and cook rapidly for about 5 minutes until quite thick.

Add the spinach and stir in the salt, ground cumin, and chilli powder. Simmer, stirring, for ten minutes.

Now add the cheese cubes and garam masala and continue to cook over a gentle heat for a further 5 minutes. Serve.

MIXED VEGETABLES

Use any combination of carrots, peas, potatoes, cauliflower, and green beans. Left-over cooked vegetables are suitable for this dish.

Serves 4–6.
Preparation and cooking time: 25–30 minutes.

1 lb (450g) diced vegetables
3 tbsp vegetable oil
1½ UK cups (1 US cup/8 fl oz/200ml) curry sauce (page 20)
1 tsp salt
½ tsp turmeric
½ tsp ground coriander
½ tsp garam masala
½ tsp chilli powder
2 tsp finely chopped green coriander

Cook the vegetables in boiling salted water for 10–15 minutes until just tender. Drain.

Heat the oil in a large frying pan, pour in the curry sauce and bring it to the boil.

Cook for about 5 minutes until the sauce thickens, then turn down the heat.

Stir in the salt and all the spices and add the cooked vegetables. Stir well and cook for 5 minutes.

Sprinkle with the green coriander just before serving.

11

RICE AND BIRYANIS

Menu

PLAIN BOILED RICE

PILAU RICE

PEAS PILAU

FRIED RICE

CHICKEN BIRYANI

LAMB BIRYANI

PRAWN BIRYANI

VEGETABLE BIRYANI

FRUITY PILAU

COOKING RICE

My friends and customers are always telling me of their difficulty in cooking rice well. I must confess that this is one area where I once experienced considerable problems myself. Now that I can cook rice perfectly, I realize my previous failures, and undoubtedly those of my friends and customers, were due to inaccurate instructions which suggested using too much water. The rice invariably ends up being soggy and mushy and the person cooking it thinks it is his or her fault. It clearly is not, as you will see.

For perfect results follow my recipes carefully and remember a few simple rules:

1. Always wash the rice in several changes of water. This removes the starch left over from the milling process and helps to keep the grains separate during cooking.
2. Always drain the rice in a colander for about 20 minutes until the grains are dry.
3. Use a heavy saucepan with a tight-fitting lid, or cover the pan with a sheet of aluminium foil before replacing the lid.
4. Cook rice on a very low heat.
5. Always finish off in a preheated oven gas mark 3 (325°F or 170°C), for about 20 minutes.
6. When stirring rice, always do so gently, using a fork to avoid breaking the grains.

Indian restaurants use basmati rice, which, although more expensive than other varieties, has the right nutty aroma to complement our curries, in addition to being well suited for the sweet rice dishes popular in India.

PLAIN BOILED RICE

Quick and easy to prepare, this is the simplest of all the rice dishes.

Serves 4.
Preparation and cooking time: 25–30 minutes.

3 UK pints (3¾ US pints/1.7 litres) water (approximately)
2 UK cups (1¼ US cups) basmati rice
1 tsp salt

Pour the water into a large pot and bring to the boil on a high heat.

Meanwhile, pick over the rice and wash in several changes of water. Drain.

Add the rice and salt to the boiling water and bring back to the boil. Turn down the heat and stir.

Simmer the rice, uncovered, for 20 minutes, stirring occasionally.

In the meantime, heat the oven to gas mark 3 (350°F or 170°C).

Drain into a large sieve, pour over cold water to remove excess starch and shake the sieve to remove as much water as possible.

Return the rice to the pot and place in the oven for about 10 minutes to dry the grains.

NB. If you are not serving the rice immediately, allow it to drain in the sieve until cool (do not place in the oven) and refrigerate. Reheat when required in a microwave oven or covered in a conventional one.

PILAU RICE

This colourful rice dish with its wonderful aroma is probably the most popular way of serving rice in Indian restaurants. It is a modification of the lavish pulaos made with lashings of ghee, opulently flavoured with saffron and generously garnished with almonds, sultanas, and silver 'vark' that are served in parts of northern India on festive occasions.

The dish familiar nowadays uses less ghee and relies on food colourings rather than the expensive saffron for its array of colours.

Serves 4.
Preparation and cooking time: about 30 minutes.

¼ tsp yellow food colouring
¼ tsp red food colouring
2 UK cups (1¼ US cups) basmati rice
1 tbsp vegetable ghee
2 tsp finely chopped onion
6 green cardamoms
1 x 2 inch (5cm) stick cinnamon
4 cloves
2 bay leaves
3 UK cups (2 US cups/15 fl oz/425ml) cold water
½ tsp salt

Mix each food colouring with about a tablespoonful of water, keeping the two colours separate, and set aside.

Pick over the rice carefully for any stones and wash thoroughly in several changes of water. Leave to drain in a colander or large sieve.

Meanwhile, heat the ghee in a heavy pot, and fry the onion until just translucent. Add the cardamoms, cinnamon, cloves, and bay leaves and cook for 1 minute.

Add the rice to the pot and mix well to coat all the grains with the ghee.

Pour in the water, add the salt, stir and bring to the boil. Once boiling, turn the heat to very low and cover the pot with a tight-fitting lid.

Switch on the oven to preheat to gas mark 3 (350°F or 170°C).

After 5 minutes stir the rice gently with a fork or a wooden spoon. Cover again for a further 3 minutes.

After this time stir the rice again, but very carefully to avoid breaking the grains which will by now have become softer. The best way to do this is to slide the spoon down the side of the pot and gently lift the rice at the bottom to the top. Cover again, and repeat this procedure after a further 2 minutes. This method ensures that all the rice cooks evenly and you don't get a soggy mass at the bottom of the pot whilst the top layer remains under-cooked.

Now take one of the food colourings and make two lines of colour across the rice. Repeat with the other food colouring and make two lines down.

Replace the lid and place the pot in the oven for 15–20 minutes to finish cooking the rice and set the colours.

Remove the rice from the oven and transfer to a suitable container layer by layer to avoid breaking the rice. Fluff up gently with a fork to distribute the coloured grains equally.

Serve immediately or cool as quickly as possible and refrigerate for no more than one day.

When reheating, the ideal way is to use the microwave oven. For 3–4 servings, heat for 2 minutes on High.

If using a conventional oven, remember to cover the rice to prevent it drying up.

PEAS PILAU

The restaurant method of making peas pilau is to warm up ready-made pilau rice (page 102) with some frozen peas that have been thawed out in a little hot oil. You may wish to do just this if you have some left-over pilau rice. If not, follow this recipe, which I feel is the better way to make this rice dish. It's delicious eaten cold with spiced yogurt (page 115).

Serves 4.
Preparation and cooking time: about 30 minutes.

2 UK cups (1¼ US cups) basmati rice
1 tbsp vegetable ghee
1 small onion, finely chopped
8 oz (225g) frozen peas
4 green cardamoms
2 bay leaves
1 x 2 inch (5cm) stick cinnamon
1 tsp whole cumin seeds
3 UK cups (2 US cups/15 fl oz/425ml) cold water
1 tsp salt

Pick over the rice and wash in several changes of water. Leave to drain in a colander or sieve.

Heat the ghee in a heavy pot and fry the onion until transparent.

Add all the remaining ingredients except the rice, water and salt, and cook on a gentle heat for 6–7 minutes, stirring now and again.

Add the drained rice and mix well. Stir in the water and salt and bring to the boil.

Cover the pot with a tight-fitting lid and turn down the heat to very low.

Preheat the oven to gas mark 3 (350°F or 170°C).

After 5 minutes stir the rice. Replace the lid for a further 3 minutes. Stir very carefully after this time by sliding the spoon down the side of the pot and gently pushing the rice at the bottom towards the top.

Place the covered pot in the hot oven for about 15 minutes to dry off the rice. Transfer to another container layer by layer and fluff up with a fork.

If not using immediately, cool, and keep covered in the refrigerator for up to a day.

FRIED RICE

This is a tasty variation of a simple rice dish. Use half of the boiled rice from page 101 to create two different rice dishes in moments.

Serves 2.
Preparation and cooking time: 5–10 minutes.

2 tbsp vegetable ghee
½ small onion, finely chopped
1 UK cup (⅔ US cup) basmati rice, boiled (page 101)

Heat the ghee in a pan and fry the onion until just beginning to brown.

Warm the rice in a microwave for about 1½ minutes, then add to the pan. Toss around in the pan for a minute or two.

Serve immediately.

BIRYANIS

Consisting of layers of cooked rice and meat, traditionally biryanis are served on grand festive occasions when they are always made with generous helpings of ghee and perfumed with saffron. Nowadays, particularly in restaurant cooking, vegetable ghee, oil, and food colourings are substituted for these rather expensive ingredients.

A biryani is a meal in itself, although for those with a healthy appetite, a yogurt dish or a vegetable side dish may make a good addition.

The recipes here are for meat or fish biryanis but vegetables may be substituted to make a vegetarian meal.

CHICKEN BIRYANI

Serves 4.
Preparation and cooking time: about 10 minutes.

1 lb (450g) cooked chicken (page 49)
2 tbsp vegetable oil
1 tbsp cashew nuts, finely chopped
1 tbsp sultanas
4 UK cups (2½ US cups) pilau rice
4 UK cups (2½ US cups/20 fl oz/550ml) curry sauce (page 20)
1 tsp garam masala
1 tsp chilli powder (or to taste)
½ tsp salt

Divide each chicken piece into two smaller pieces and set them aside.

Heat the oil in a deep frying pan. When hot, add the nuts and stir around until they turn light golden in colour. Remove with a slotted spoon and spread them out on a plate lined with kitchen paper.

Drop the sultanas into the same hot oil. They will plump up in a second or two. Remove immediately and put them on the same plate as the nuts.

Now put the chicken pieces into the pan and stir. Turn down the heat to very low.

Warm the rice for about 2 minutes in a microwave oven. Add to the chicken.

Stir very gently to avoid breaking the grains. Heat for 2 or 3 minutes tossing the rice and chicken rather than stirring.

Put the rice and chicken in a serving dish and keep warm.

Pour the curry sauce into a clean pan and bring to a simmer. Stir in the garam masala, chilli powder, and salt.

Pour the sauce into serving dishes, sprinkle the biryani with the nuts and sultanas and serve.

LAMB BIRYANI

Follow the recipe for Chicken Biryani on page 107, substituting the chicken with the same quantity of cooked lamb.

PRAWN BIRYANI

Follow the recipe for Chicken Biryani on page 107, replacing the chicken with about 12 oz (350g) of prawns cooked in a little hot oil for 3 to 4 minutes.

VEGETABLE BIRYANI

Follow the recipe for Chicken Biryani on page 107, but use about 12 oz (350g) diced cooked vegetables of your choice instead of the chicken.

FRUITY PILAU

The sultanas and almonds in this dish add a nice touch of decadence and sweetness, really good when served with a spicy curry.

Serves 4.
Preparation and cooking time: about 30 minutes.

2 UK cups (1¼ US cups) basmati rice
1 tbsp unsalted butter or ghee
1 bay leaf
6 cardamom pods
1 stick of cinnamon, about 2 inches (5cm) in length
6 whole black peppercorns
3 tbsp sultanas
1 tbsp flaked almonds
3 UK cups (2 US cups/15 fl oz/425ml) cold water
1 tsp salt

Wash the rice well and set aside in a sieve to drain.

Heat the butter or ghee in a heavy-based saucepan on a low heat until melted. Add the bay leaf, cardamoms, cinnamon stick and peppercorns and stir for about 30 seconds.

Add the rice, sultanas and almonds, mix well and stir fry gently for about a minute. Now add the water and salt, mix and bring to the boil.

Preheat the oven to gas mark 3 (350°F or 170°C).

Cover the pan with a tight-fitting lid, turn the heat down to as low as it will go and leave for about 5 minutes. Stir, cover again and leave for another 5 minutes.

Place the pan in the warm oven for about 15 minutes to finish cooking. Remove carefully, fluff up the rice with a fork and serve hot.

12

YOGURTS AND
YOGURT DRINKS

Menu

CUCUMBER RAITA

RAITA WITH RADISH

SPICED YOGURT

YOGURT FLAVOURED WITH GARLIC AND CUMIN

YOGURT DRINKS

LASSI

YOGURT

If your experience of yogurt has been limited to the shop-bought variety, then the taste of home-made yogurt will surprise you. It is much less tart and so much more pleasant that even when eaten plain it is very palatable. Add a few spices and vegetables to it and it becomes delicious.

In India the goodness and versatility of yogurt is exploited to the full. Its versatility is demonstrated by the wide variety of uses such as for sauces, marinades, as a lightener in breads, or as an accompaniment to meals sweetened or spiced. Nutritionally, yogurt is rich in protein and is easier to digest than milk, having the necessary flora for a healthy digestion. It is little wonder that Indian homes are seldom without it and that it is served with almost every meal.

Indian restaurants use yogurt mainly as a marinade to tenderize meat and fish. Although it is offered as a side dish on the menu, few people ask for it. I believe this is because Westerners are not familiar with yogurt as part of a main meal, being more used to eating it sweetened and then only if health- or diet-conscious. This is a pity, and I would urge you to try some of my recipes as I am convinced you will like them.

Yogurt is particularly good eaten with rice or parathas as a main meal, or as a cooling side dish with the more 'dry' curries and bhajis.

HOW TO MAKE YOGURT

To make yogurt at home you will need some milk and a little live yogurt. You may use full cream milk, semi-skimmed or skimmed milk, or even soya milk if you prefer. Full cream milk will obviously result in a creamier yogurt which is nicer for eating but skimmed or semi-skimmed also produce a good result, particularly if you follow my suggestion of adding a little skimmed milk powder to the warm milk.

The live yogurt or 'starter' that is added to warm milk requires continuing warmth to allow the culture in the starter to grow and turn the milk into yogurt. I have never used a thermometer for this purpose, relying on my own perception but, should you need to do so, a temperature between 30°C–38°C (85°F–100°F) is ideal. Much warmer than this and the milk will curdle. Much cooler and it will not set.

After adding the starter to the milk, it needs to be kept warm for a few hours to allow the culture to do its work. In the restaurant we would place the pot on top of the tandoor once it had been closed down, with the glowing embers still keeping the tandoor warm, and wrap the pot in several tea towels to hold in the heat. At home a warm airing cupboard is just as suitable.

If you really have a taste for home-made yogurt, it is worth investing in a yogurt maker. I use one at home and find this to be the easiest and most convenient way of making yogurt.

You will require:

1 UK pint (1¼ US pints/570ml) milk
1 tbsp live plain yogurt
2 tbsp skimmed milk powder (optional)

Bring the milk to the boil in a saucepan. Cover and leave to cool until warm to the touch. If using a thermometer, around 40°C (105°F) is ideal.

Beat the yogurt with a spoon until smooth and mix it into the milk, stirring in the skin that will have formed on top of the milk. Also stir in the skimmed milk powder if using.

Warm a bowl or any suitable non-metallic container and pour in the milk. Cover and wrap with towels or an old shawl.

Set aside in a warm place as suggested for around 4–6 hours.

Refrigerate the yogurt until required. It will keep in perfect condition for up to 5 days.

Tip: Removing the yogurt as quickly as possible after it has set will result in a sweeter yogurt, ideal for eating. If you are planning to use the yogurt for marinating purposes only, leave it an hour or two after it has set to make it more tart.

CUCUMBER RAITA

This is a delicious, cooling yogurt dish, excellent served with spicy curries together with rice and/or Indian breads.

Serves 4.
Preparation time: 5 minutes.

1 UK pint (1¼ US pints/570ml) plain yogurt
1 tsp salt
4 inch (10cm) piece of cucumber
½ tsp garam masala
Freshly ground black pepper

Put the yogurt and salt into a bowl and beat with a fork until smooth.

Thinly slice the cucumber, place the slices on top of each other and cut into strips. Now cut the strips into dice. Scatter over the yogurt.

Cover and refrigerate until required. Sprinkle on the garam masala and black pepper just before serving.

NB. Allow the yogurt to reach room temperature before serving.

RAITA WITH RADISH

This raita has more bite than cucumber raita and is delicious eaten on its own as well as with rice and curries. The radish used in this recipe is known as *mooli*. This is white in colour and shaped rather like a large carrot. It is sweeter in taste than the well-known smaller red radishes and is excellent in salads. Moolis are now readily available in supermarkets as well as Asian greengrocers. If you cannot get them, use whatever radish you can find.

Serves 4.
Preparation time: 5 minutes.

1 UK pint (1¼ US pints/570ml) plain yogurt
1 tsp salt
5 inch (13cm) piece mooli
½ tsp garam masala
1 green chilli, finely chopped

Put the yogurt and salt into a bowl and beat with a fork until smooth.

Peel, wash, and grate the mooli. Add to the yogurt together with the garam masala and the chilli.

Mix and refrigerate until required.

SPICED YOGURT

This is a simple yogurt dish that can be served with any meal.

Serves 4.
Preparation time: 2–3 minutes.

1 UK pint (1¼ US pints/570ml) plain yogurt
4 tbsp milk
1 tsp salt
½ tsp garam masala
½ tsp chilli powder

Put all the ingredients into a bowl and mix thoroughly. Cover and refrigerate until ready to serve.

YOGURT FLAVOURED WITH GARLIC AND CUMIN

The combination of garlic and cumin flavours is quite unusual in a yogurt dish, but the wonderful taste of this preparation only serves to illustrate the wide variety of ingredients that can be successfully added to yogurt.

Serves 4.
Preparation time: 4–5 minutes.

1 UK pint (1¼ US pints/570ml) plain yogurt
1 tsp salt
1 small clove of garlic
½–1 green chilli, finely chopped
1 tsp whole cumin
2 tsp finely chopped onion
Pinch of turmeric

Put the yogurt and salt into a bowl and beat with a fork until smooth and creamy.

Crush the garlic using a garlic press or chop very finely.

Add to the yogurt, together with the remaining ingredients and mix.

Serve immediately or keep in the refrigerator until required.

YOGURT DRINKS

Even now in modern India, many people keep livestock for milk. Milking takes place very early each morning. Towards the end of the day, the milk that remains after the day's requirements is boiled, cooled, and poured into large clay urns which are left overnight to produce yogurt for the following day. The important task of churning the yogurt to make butter (makhan) is undertaken with great enthusiasm at the crack of dawn. Some of the makhan is eaten as it is with yogurt and breads and the rest is heated and clarified to make ghee. The liquid that is left after churning the yogurt and removing the makhan is the lassi.

Lassi is a refreshing and nutritious drink that is served throughout the heat of the day and also with meals instead of water.

I do not expect you to go through this lengthy process in order to enjoy home-made lassi, so you will find the following method quick, simple, and perfectly acceptable.

LASSI (SWEET OR SOUR)

Makes almost 1 UK pint (1¼ US pints/570ml).
Preparation and cooking time: 2–3 minutes.

2 UK cups (1¼ US cups/10 fl oz/275ml) plain yogurt
2 UK cups (1¼ US cups/10 fl oz/275ml) cold water
½ tsp salt (for sour lassi)
Freshly ground black pepper (optional for sour lassi)
2 tsp sugar (for sweet lassi)

Place all the ingredients in a bowl and whisk until frothy. Serve in tall glasses with plenty of ice.

13

SWEETS

Menu

KULFI

MANGOES

TROPICAL FRUIT SALAD

GULAB JAMONS

KULFI

Kulfi is sometimes known as Indian ice cream. I have tried many varieties of kulfi throughout the country; this recipe produces by far the best I have ever eaten.

Serves 8.
Preparation and cooking time: about 1½ hours.

4 UK pints (5 US pints/2.25 litres) whole milk
12 green cardamoms
10 tbsp granulated sugar
3 tbsp flaked almonds
2 UK cups (1¼ US cups/10 fl oz/275ml) single cream
2 tbsp finely chopped unsalted pistachios

Bring the milk to the boil in a heavy pot. Turn down the heat to allow the milk to simmer vigorously without boiling over.

The milk must reduce considerably, to about one third of its original amount. Stir frequently as the milk simmers, incorporating the skin that forms on the top, and scrape and stir in the milk that dries and sticks to the sides of the pot.

While the milk is simmering, take the seeds out of the cardamom pods and grind finely. Stir them into the milk.

When the milk has reduced sufficiently, stir in the sugar and the almonds. Simmer for 2–3 minutes until the sugar dissolves completely.

Take the milk off the heat and allow it to cool slightly. Stir in the cream and half the pistachios.

Pour it into a square or rectangular vessel that will allow the mixture to sit 2–3 inches (5–7.5cm) deep. Cool completely. Cover and place in the freezer for about 30 minutes. Sprinkle over the remaining pistachios and return to the freezer until set. Remove the kulfi from the freezer 15 minutes before serving and cut into ½ inch (1cm) cubes.

MANGOES

Fresh mangoes are amongst the finest fruits in the world. Soft, sweet, ripe mangoes make an excellent dessert, fit for any occasion.

When buying fresh mangoes, look for those with a strong mango aroma, and a clear yellow skin with reddish patches. Ripe fruits should also yield slightly when squeezed. A mango has a large stone. To serve, cut this out and either peel and cut into slices or (and this is the method used in most restaurants) cut the fruit in half along its length, leaving the skin on. Cut out the stone, and turn the fruit inside out revealing the flesh uppermost. Make slits in the flesh, right down to the skin, lengthwise about ½ inch (1cm) apart and then crosswise to create a 'hedgehog'.

TROPICAL FRUIT SALAD

Served chilled this is an exotic and refreshing sweet, ideal after a spicy meal.

We always used canned fruits for this as they are very good but you may like to try it with fresh fruits as they are readily available from most supermarkets.

Serves 6–8.

1 can of sliced mangoes
1 can of guavas
1 can of lychees

Drain about half the syrup out of each can and combine all the fruit in a salad bowl.

Chill for at least half an hour before serving.

GULAB JAMONS

These are very light, soft, sponge-like sweets soaked in a light, flavoured syrup. They are easy to make and a delicious conclusion to a spicy meal. Serve warm or cold.

Allow three to four per person and sprinkle with a little brandy for a really special sweet.

Makes 16.
Preparation and cooking time: about 30 minutes.

For syrup:
8 oz (225g) granulated sugar
6 green cardamoms
4 UK cups (2½ US cups/20 fl oz/550ml) cold water

For jamons:
6 tbsp full fat milk powder
2 tbsp self-raising flour
1 tbsp melted butter
A little cold milk to bind
Oil for deep frying

Put the sugar, cardamoms, and water into a pot and bring to the boil. Turn down the heat and simmer the syrup for about 15 minutes.

Meanwhile, sift the milk powder and flour into a bowl. Add the melted butter and rub into the mixture with fingertips until it resembles fine breadcrumbs.

Add the milk a little at a time, drawing in the mixture to form a soft dough.

Heat the oil in a pan or karahi and divide the dough into 16 parts. Roll each one out in the palms of your hands into a little ball.

The syrup should be ready by now. Take it off the heat so that it may cool slightly before having the jamons put into it.

Test the oil by putting in one ball of dough. The oil must only just be hot enough to make the dough rise to the surface after a few seconds and to fry it very gently. Adjust as necessary.

When the oil is at the right heat, put in as many balls of dough as your pan or karahi will easily take.

Move the pan about carefully to keep the jamons moving until they rise to the surface of the oil.

When they are at the surface, keep moving them about with a slotted spoon to ensure that they cook evenly.

The jamons will almost double in size as they are cooking and will turn a deep, golden brown colour. This should take about 4–5 minutes.

Drain on kitchen paper, allow to cool for 5 minutes and drop them into the syrup.

The jamons will be very soft and easily broken until they have cooled, when the texture will become firmer.

Serve with a few tablespoonfuls of the syrup for each person.

INDEX

Now available, the sequel to *The Curry Secret*:

THE NEW CURRY SECRET
Mouthwatering Indian Restaurant Dishes to Cook at Home

A new 192-page book from Kris Dhillon containing 100 brand-new recipes and illustrated with 61 colour photographs.

As each year passes, more and more new and vibrant recipes are served in Indian restaurants. In *The New Curry Secret* Kris Dhillon shows how to create these wonderful new dishes easily and expertly. The mouthwatering recipes include Chicken Chettinad, Lamb Kalia, Balti Subzi, Beef Badami, Fish Ambotik, Malabar Prawn Biryani, to name just a few. Plus there are labour-saving ideas and tips to make cooking your favourite Indian restaurant food at home even easier.